Camden Town Advanced

YOUNG PEOPLE
Going global in the digital age
Introduction to advanced English skills

Erarbeitet von

Stephanie Claussen
Pamela Hanus
Christoph Reuter
Mirja Schnoor
Sylvia Wauer

Diesterweg

© 2014 Bildungshaus Schulbuchverlage
Westermann Schroedel Diesterweg Schöningh Winklers GmbH, Braunschweig
www.diesterweg.de

Das Werk und seine Teile sind urheberrechtlich geschützt. Jede Nutzung in anderen als den gesetzlich zugelassenen Fällen bedarf der vorherigen schriftlichen Einwilligung des Verlages. Hinweis zu §52a UrhG: Weder das Werk noch seine Teile dürfen ohne eine solche Einwilligung gescannt und in ein Netzwerk eingestellt werden. Das gilt auch für Intranets von Schulen und sonstigen Bildungseinrichtungen.
Auf verschiedenen Seiten dieses Buches befinden sich Verweise (Links) auf Internet-Adressen.
Haftungshinweis: Trotz sorgfältiger inhaltlicher Kontrolle wird die Haftung für die Inhalte der externen Seiten ausgeschlossen. Für den Inhalt dieser externen Seiten sind ausschließlich deren Betreiber verantwortlich. Sollten Sie bei dem angegebenen Inhalt des Anbieters dieser Seite auf kostenpflichtige, illegale oder anstößige Inhalte treffen, so bedauern wir dies ausdrücklich und bitten Sie, uns umgehend per E-Mail davon in Kenntnis zu setzen, damit beim Nachdruck der Verweis gelöscht wird.

Druck A[1] / Jahr 2014
Alle Drucke der Serie A sind im Unterricht parallel verwendbar.

Redaktion: Daniel Harnett, Demet Kömür und Daniel Shatwell unter Mitarbeit von Charlotte Finn
Layoutkonzeption: Druckreif! Sandra Grünberg, Braunschweig
Illustrationen: Oliver Fuchs, Berlin
Umschlaggestaltung: blum DESIGN & KOMMUNIKATION GmbH, Hamburg
Satz: Konrad Triltsch GmbH, Ochsenfurth
Druck und Bindung: westermann druck GmbH, Braunschweig

ISBN 978-3-425-**74014**-8

Contents

Part 1: Going places – Living, learning and working abroad

Page	Theme	Text types	Skills training

1 Time out: Spending a gap year abroad

Page	Theme	Text types	Skills training
6	**A Getting started** Year abroad experiences	• email • video clip	

8	**B Practice section**	• newspaper article
		 • letter
			• Writing: Summary
			 • Analyzing a newspaper article:
			   – facts vs. opinion
			   – rhetorical strategies/devices
			 • Writing: A letter to the editor

15	**C Getting to the point**	• newspaper article	
18	**D Listening**	• news video • email	• Listening/viewing

2 Choices choices choices: Applying to study and work abroad

Page	Theme	Text types	Skills training
22	**A Getting started** Applying for jobs abroad	• video clip • advertisement	

26	**B Practice section**	• job advertisement
		 • covering letter
		 • curriculum vitae
			• Writing:
			   – a covering letter
			   – a curriculum vitae

30	**C Speaking**	• monologue: talk
		 • video clip
		 • job advertisements
		 • dialogue: job interview
			• Giving feedback
			 • Speaking:
			   – giving a talk about jobs
			   – conducting a job interview
			 • Listening: note taking

42	**D Mediation**	• newspaper article	• Writing: – an email explaining a German newspaper article to a student from the USA

3 Neither here nor there: Living in a multicultural society

Page	Theme	Text types	Skills training
48	**A Getting started** Talking about aspects of identity		

50	**B Practice section**	• novel
		 • extract
			• Analyzing fictional texts:
			   – characterization
			   – narrative perspective
			 • Creative writing: Writing a dialogue from a different point of view

58	**C Getting to the point**	• novel • extract	• Creative writing: Re-telling a story from a different narrative perspective

Contents

Part 2: Living in the digital world

Page	Theme	Text types	Skills training

4 Think before you post: Dangers of the Internet

Page	Theme	Text types	Skills training
60	A Getting started Talking about the use of the Internet and the dangers involved	• cartoon • novel	

62	B Practice section	• cartoon
		• newspaper comment
			• Analyzing cartoons
			• Analyzing non-fictional texts
			  – identifying point of view
			  – rhetorical devices
			  – detecting bias

67	C Getting to the point	• cartoon • newspaper article	

5 (Anti-)social network: Media and friendship

Page	Theme	Text types	Skills training
70	A Getting started Talking about the development and the significance of Facebook	• statistics • newspaper comment	• Analyzing statistics • Speaking: Holding a debate
72	B Practice section	• film excerpts • newspaper article	• Analyzing film
79	C Getting to the point		

80	D Speaking	• monologue
		• dialogue
			• Speaking:
			  – explaining graphs
			  – explaining cartoons
			  – talking about social networks
			• Giving feedback
			• Speaking: Discussing a topic with a partner

6 A question of gender: Sexual identity

Page	Theme	Text types	Skills training
88	A Getting started: Talking about aspects of sexual identity	• drama	
90	B Practice section	• drama	• Analyzing drama • Creative writing: Continuing a scene
95	C Getting to the point	• drama	
98	D Listening	• podcast	• Listening • Writing: A speech

Contents

Part 3: Visions and values in the global village

Page	Theme	Text types	Skills training

7 A (brave) new world: What will the future bring?

Page	Theme	Text types	Skills training
100	A Getting started: Talking about visions of the future	• novel • film	
102	B Practice section	• novel extract	• Analyzing fictional texts: – atmosphere – use of language
107	C Getting to the point	• novel extract	• Comment: Discussing if a vision of the future is relevant today

8 Paying the price: Global fashion

Page	Theme	Text types	Skills training
110	A Getting started: Talking about the cost of global fashion	• video clip • infographics/statistics	
113	B Practice section	• video clip • blog excerpt	• Listening/viewing • Analyzing a non-fictional text: – choice of words – imagery
119	C Getting to the point	• podcast • blog entry	• listening
121	D Mediation		• Writing: Drafting a report based on a German-language source

Page	
6	Themes 1–8
124	Skills
153	Glossary – Literary terms
164	Glossary – Alphabetical

1 Time out

Getting started

A1 a) Imagine you have just passed your final exams. Where do you go from here? Write down your plans for the immediate future.

b) Discuss your plans with a partner and talk about similarities and differences.

A2 A lot of young people choose to take a gap year after school. They spend some time travelling around the world, often to work or volunteer, but also to enjoy themselves. Here are three extracts from e-mail messages that gap year travellers (or "gappers") wrote home to their families.

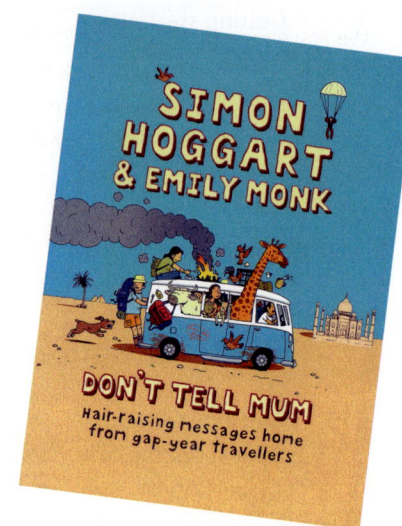

a) Read the extracts. Summarize the gappers' different experiences.

b) Talk to a partner about how you would have felt and how well you would have coped in these situations.

c) Describe the image of "gap year" and "gappers" that is conveyed in the e-mails.

1.

This young student spent a year in northern Russia improving her language skills. The winter of 2005–6 was one of the coldest ever recorded there.

[1] **to lobotomize** = to remove a part of so.'s brain by a medical operation
[2] **habitat** = the area or environment in which so./sth. normally lives or grows
[3] **High St Ken.** = High Street Kensington in London
[4] **octogenarian** = a person between 80 and 90 years of age
[5] **babushka** = Russian: old woman, grandmother
[6] **felt slipper** = Filzpantoffel
[7] **turnip** = Rübe
[8] **frostbite** = a medical condition in which cold weather seriously damages your fingers, toes, ears or nose

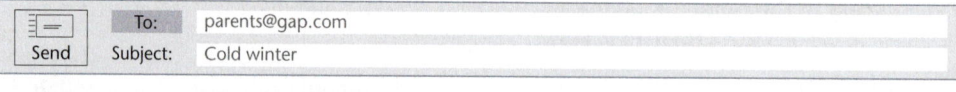

To: parents@gap.com
Subject: Cold winter

I know it is v dull to talk about the weather, but it is MINUS 30 degrees today, so I think I am allowed. All my shampoo on my shelf etc. freezes every night and children aren't allowed to go to school because they walk too slowly and tend to freeze to death before they get there. Nice. I am slightly worried as I walk at the speed of a lobotomized[1] snail, there is 5 inches of ice on the
5 roads and my new boots have strayed far from their natural habitat[2] (the wilds of High St Ken.[3]). On the first day of unbelievable iciness I happily stepped outside and within minutes my mascara had frozen my eyelids closed and my nostrils had iced over, after another few minutes I lost all feeling in my extremities, so by the time I reached the Institute I couldn't see, smell or feel.
10 I walk so slowly that I am often overtaken by octogenarian[4] babushkas[5] shuffling along in felt slippers[6] with massive sacks of turnips[7] on their backs. Every day Ludmilla smugly informs me that it is another 10 degrees colder than the day before and happily tells me how to notice the first stages of frostbite[8].

2.

Politics rarely intrudes into the lives of our gappers, but when it does, it can be embarrassing. Imagine that your child was in Nepal and they reported back that everything was just fine – except that they had been seized by a group of revolutionary guerrillas.

To: parents@gap.com
Subject: What an experience!

We first encountered the Maoists about a month into the placement. Somewhere along the line what actually happened got a bit distorted. To say we were held hostage[1] would be overshooting the mark[2], although technically it's true. We all went to get the 11 a.m. bus into Ghorabi, and as we approached the place where the bus sits and waits we were surrounded by six men, none older than us, brandishing[3] 1960's Kalashnikov rifles[4]. They told us to sit down (we did) and that we were not allowed to leave until the rally[5], which we had inadvertently stumbled upon, was finished.
It was scary, they were painfully young and they had guns which they chose to point at us. So for four hours we sat and listened and watched while these Maoists preached their message to the masses. After the initial fear wore off, it simply became a bit boring. We couldn't understand what was being said, and it lasted a long time. When it was finished we walked home, and that was that.

[1] **to be held hostage** = als Geisel gehalten werden
[2] **to overshoot the mark** = über das Ziel hinausschießen
[3] **to brandish** = to wave a weapon around in your hand
[4] **rifle** = a large gun
[5] **rally** = a gathering, a public meeting intended to inspire enthusiasm for a cause

3.

This young woman is a volunteer in Kenya and accompanies her pupils to an inter-school music competition:

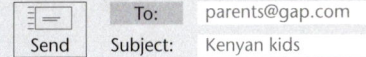

To: parents@gap.com
Subject: Kenyan kids

Next to the other school, our primary children look like a Kenyan version of the Bash Street Kids[1]. The neatness of the other competitors only made us more fiercely loyal to our little darlings, and the music teacher, Mr Wafula, said that we sounded like a hundred people cheering rather than three. I was also filled with maternal[2] pride when they came second, a feeling which surprised me as I spend most of my lessons confiscating ingenious catapults made from a hollow biro and an elastic band, unsticking small children from the wall in art lessons, or avoiding eagerly offered snotty hands.
They are also getting bolder and wander into the house without warning. This means it's not unusual to come out of the bedroom wearing nothing but a towel to find three small children in the kitchen trying to take apart the gas stove. I'm doing reading lessons to help a 4-year-old called Tracey, and it's going well. You may think that Tracey is an odd Kenyan name, but I teach Wayne, Brenda, Maureen, Kelvin, Brian and Eric. I'm also helping with a national art competition, although I had to explain to Mr Okingo that 'helping' was not the same as 'doing 20 entries myself and getting the children to write their names at the bottom', which is what he wanted me to do.

[1] **Bash Street Kids** = an ongoing comic strip in the British comic *The Beano*
[2] **maternal** = of a mother

A3 In 2010, the Youtube sketch video "Gap Yah" gained widespread popularity. It features Orlando on the phone to his friend Tarquin talking about his gap-year experiences in Tanzania, Peru and Burma. His pronunciation, especially the use of the long vowel "ah", identifies him as a member of the upper class.

Watch the sketch and note down what aspects of "gappers" and the gap-year experience the sketch makes fun of.   www.diesterweg.de/cta/74014/links

chunder = to vomit, be sick

A4 Pair work: Prepare and perform a role play with the following two roles:
- A student who wants to persuade his/her parents to let him/her go on a gap year.
- His/her worried parent who would prefer him/her to stay at home.

1 Time out: Spending a gap year abroad

Practice section

Pre-reading

B1 Read the heading of the article from The *Guardian* and speculate on what it is about.

Patrick Kingsley   The Guardian, 6 September, 2010

Gap years: Wasted youth?

Ever wondered what students really get up to on their gap years?
A report from the Full Moon Party in Thailand

Outside the Drop In bar on Kho Phangan, Thailand, 25 August 2010.
Photograph for the Guardian by Sean Smith

[1] **epitome** = the best possible example of a particluar type of person or thing
[2] **pinnacle** = *here:* the most exciting part of so.'s life
[3] **chief executive** = the most senior manager in a company or organization
[4] **UCAS** = Universities and Colleges Admissions Service = an organization responsible for managing applications to almost all UK universities and colleges

Up and down the beach, young western men are unzipping their shorts and peeing into the Gulf of Thailand. Behind them, under the light of the full moon, thousands more shirtless, shoeless Europeans are massed outside 14 beachside bars, their knees bending awkwardly to a soundtrack of the Black Eyed Peas, Justin Bieber and generic drum'n'bass. And squeezed between the bars and the crowds are 35 wooden stalls, each selling plastic buckets filled with a litre's worth of vodka and Red Bull. The stalls are daubed with deeply dubious slogans, ranging from the lurid to the moronic. "No Bucket No Boom Boom", "Fuck My Buckets", "Everybody Fuck My Strong Buckets" – that kind of thing.

Welcome to the Full Moon Party, the largest beach rave in the world. Twenty-five years ago, this was a little-known hippy hang-out on the remote Thai island of Koh Phangan. Today, frequented every month by between 10,000 and 30,000 European youngsters, the all-night party is the ultimate destination on south-east Asia's "banana pancake" trail; a mecca for footloose gap-year tourists. This party scene, right here on this beach, is arguably the epitome[1], the pinnacle[2], of the modern gap-year experience. Three weeks ago, the chief executive[3] of the universities and colleges admissions service (UCAS)[4] declared to a Sunday newspaper that "the golden age of the gap year is over". Mary

Comprehension

B2 Read the article and check whether your speculations were right.

Curnock Cook argued that while in the past "a gap year has been when young people take a nice break and go out and see the world", the period should now "be used in a focused way to support an application to the course or university you are targeting". In a year when the number of university applications – a record 660,000 – has dwarfed[5] the number of university places available – 450,000 – Curnock Cook may have a point.

But this is a point that has yet to trickle down, in practical terms, to the nation's school-leavers. In fact, the vast majority of gappers do not use their year-out in anything approaching a fashion that might – in the eyes of universities – be viewed as "constructive". Every year around 160,000 British school-leavers take a gap year before entering university. More than 80% of them, says Richard Oliver, chairman of trustees at Year Out, "just go off and travel independently without any real purpose. Sun, sand and sangria, as I call it." Indeed, the trend might even be away from the year of constructive good deeds that Curnock Cook might be thinking of – a trend towards increasingly mindless hedonism. [...]

Attempting to understand why they go, however, why this is the modern gap-year experience, is exactly what brings me to the Full Moon Party, surrounded by scores of topless teenagers urinating into the ocean to the words of the Black Eyed Peas' "I gotta feeling/That tonight's gonna be a good night/That tonight's gonna be a good, good night." What exactly is the lure of this beach to teenagers who are, after all, meant to be Britain's brightest? I'm here to find out. [...]

"You know what the worst thing about travelling is?" asks Londoner Jez, 19 years old, dressed in a vest, and approaching the end of his year out. He enlightens me: "TOURISTS." It's a slightly strange answer: we're sitting on the side of a dirt track near the centre of Had Rin, the main tourist town on Koh Phangan, and venue for tomorrow's Full Moon Party. Tourists are whizzing past every 30 seconds on mopeds belching out acrid fumes. [...] But Jez – a warm, welcoming guy – doesn't think of himself as a tourist: he's a backpacker. "Most of the people here are backpackers," he insists. "Backpackers are infinitely different to tourists. [...] All the people you've met while you're travelling will be here. It's just awesome." [...] Hailey's gap-year experiences were slightly different to Jez's. She didn't go travelling at all, she says, but spent the entire period working in a hospital in order to enhance her application to medical school; a perfect exemplar of the kind of gap year favoured by Curnock Cook. In many ways, though, she wishes she'd chosen a more relaxed path. "I don't know if I should say this," she starts, pauses, then continues: "I was in a verbally abusive relationship for three years, which meant I had no self-confidence. And I turned into a bit of a slut on my gap year because I was really messed up in the head. And then I went to uni, and I thought, 'I don't want to be either of those people I've been, I want to be someone else.' So then I sort of[6] had three personalities. But coming out here on my own, having to go over and talk to people, having to be nice, not an asshole ... It's been great. It teaches you how to socialise properly. It makes you so much more confident. Coming out here, travelling on your own ..." She trails off, and then hurriedly starts again: "If I'd done the whole travelling on my own thing in my gap year, I would have been slightly less messed up[7] at uni." [...]

Up and down the beach, young western men are still unzipping their shorts and peeing into the Gulf of Thailand. Though I never took a gap year, never took the chance to either let my hair down like this, or do something more constructive, nothing that I've heard or seen here makes me want to join them.

---

[5] **to dwarf** = to make sth. seem small or unimportant
[6] **sort of** (infml) = somewhat, rather
[7] **messed up** (infml) = so. who is messed up has emotional or mental problems because unpleasant things have happened to them

1 Time out: Spending a gap year abroad

Summary: Identifying the theme

B3 a) Identifying the theme: From the sentences below, choose the one that sums up best what the article is about. Keep in mind that the sentence should not just give a brief overview, but express the main theme or problem presented in the text.

The newspaper article "Gap years: Wasted youth?" by Patrick Kingsley, published in The *Guardian* on September 6, 2010, deals with …

1. … the differences between real "gappers" and tourists.
2. … the party culture of young people going abroad for a gap year.
3. … the activities of young people in their gap year in Koh Phangan, Thailand.
4. … the question of whether young people use their gap year constructively.

b) Discuss your choices in class.

c) Look at the introductory sentences. What other information must you include in addition to the article's main theme or problem?

Summary: Outlining the structure

Checklist: Summary p. 124

B4 When you are writing the summary of a text, imagine the summary is for someone who has not read the text and needs to know the essence of what the text is about. In order to identify the main elements of an article and be able to present them more clearly, it helps to subdivide the article into meaningful parts and use those parts as a basis for the summary. A change of the topic and of the person whose views are presented (e.g. author, interviewees) can signal the beginning of a new section.

a) Outline the structure of the article.

b) Identify where the remaining parts start and end and add the line numbers. Subdivide longer parts into meaningful units where necessary. Which of the criteria mentioned above can be used to subdivide the article?

c) Make notes for each part to sum up the most important points.

ll. 1–15 Impressions of the young people's party scene in Thailand (people, music, slogans)
ll. 16–zz …

B5 Use your results from B3 and B4 to write a summary of the article "Gap year: Wasted youth?"

> **Checklist**
> ✓ Use the simple present.
> ✓ Present events in a chronological order.
> ✓ Don't quote from the text. Use your own words.
> ✓ Don't start analyzing the text.
> ✓ Don't give your personal opinion.
> ✓ Use connectives to link your sentences.

Analysis

Identifying the type of newspaper article

B6 Identify what kind of newspaper article the text is. Use the definitions below.

> **Info: Types of articles**
> *Articles can be distinguished by the way they are written and the purpose they serve.*
>
> **1. Informative articles**
> Here the main focus is on providing factual information so that the article basically provides answers to *wh*-questions such as *who, what, where, when, why* and *how*.
>
> **2. Argumentative articles**
> In such articles the author clearly intends to influence the reader and his opinion by presenting arguments that are put forward to express a particular point of view.
>
> **3. Evaluative articles**
> In such articles the author provides a critical account of an event or a topic and tends to incorporate narrative and evaluative elements.
>
> *Note:* Articles often have characteristics of more than one of the types described above.

Structure of a newspaper article

B7 Divide the article into units and identify the main function of each part.

> **Info: Structure of a newspaper article**
>
> 1. Consider the **headline** and **sub-heading** as they clarify the topic and give you a clue as to whether the article is simply informative or includes the author's interpretation of events or a form of argumentation as well.
>
> 2. Look for an **introduction**, which may include the most important information (*who, what, where, when, why, how*) or consist of a paragraph that is meant to capture the reader's attention by providing an entertaining, emotive or critical lead into the text.
>
> 3. Read the **main part** of the text. Identify the main part's structure and the function of the individual paragraphs: Is a paragraph more informative and fact-based or does it include the author's or someone else's opinion? Does the paragraph focus on facts (e.g. statistics, details of an event) or personal statements and examples?
>
> 4. Check whether there is a **concluding paragraph** that sums up the article's message or main points. Does it refer back to the beginning so that the article comes full circle?
>
> 5. Sometimes **photos, graphs** or **additional texts** may have been added to the article.

1 Time out: Spending a gap year abroad

Distinguishing between fact and opinion

B8 a) Read the text again and identify passages that express facts and opinions. Write down examples with line numbers and explain why you consider them facts or opinions.

> **Info: Facts vs. opinions**
>
> 1. An article usually contains a number of **facts**. A fact is something that is known to be true and can be proved to be so.
> 2. However, the author may also include his or her **opinion**, i.e. something that is a belief or judgement which others may or may not agree with according to their point of view.
> 3. If a text relies heavily on opinions, it is said to be **biased** and needs to be read critically.

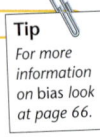

Tip
For more information on bias look at page 66.

b) Based on your findings in a), discuss whether the article is biased in the sense that the author's personal point of view is clearly stated. Describe the effect on the reader. The following questions may help you come to a conclusion:

facts	opinions
• Do the facts represent just one point of view? • How are positive and negative facts balanced out? • To what extent do you feel that some facts have been omitted on purpose? If so, which ones might those be?	• Are some opinions presented as facts? • Has the author used opinions to persuade or influence the reader in a certain way? • Are facts and opinions linked so that they add up to an overall point of view of the text?

c) Reassess what kind of newspaper article this is. Use your findings from b) for support.

Language

B9 Analyze how the use of language expresses bias or neutrality on the author's part.

Checklist:
Text analysis
p. 125

How to structure a text
pp. 138-141

> **Info: Language**
> *The reader's understanding of a topic can be influenced in many ways.*
>
> 1. **Choice of words:**
>   → use of comparatives and superlatives, e.g. "Britain's brightest (l. 65), "more constructive" (l. 112)
>   → use of strong or emotive adjectives and verbs, e.g. "dwarfed" (l. 38), "mindless" (l. 55)
>
> 2. **Register:**
>   → matter-of-fact and neutral language
>   → formal and academic language
>   → informal and colloquial language
>
> 3. **Stylistic devices:** e.g. repetition, enumeration, irony, exaggeration, metaphor
>
> 4. **Rhetorical strategies:**
>   → to quote experts and authorities or to refer to research and statistics
>   → to include personal statements of people affected by what is presented
>   → to make claims (instead of arguments based on evidence, e.g. *No one can deny that ...*)
>   → to use humour, irony, ridicule

Comment

 a) Read the letter to the editor in which a reader comments on the article "Gap year: Wasted youth?" Sum up the reader's opinion in one or two sentences.

b) Identify words and sentences that can be used in a letter to the editor and add them to the grid on page 14.

Sir or Madam,

I am writing in response to your article "Gap years: Wasted youth?" from Sep 6.

As a firm believer in (self-)discipline and order, I could not agree with the author more.

It is beyond doubt that gap years as they are conducted by today's youth really are a total waste of time and money. Your article shows precisely what is wrong with those young people: the constant partying, the hedonistic behaviour, the total lack of morals and self-control. The article raises the question whether these trips can be seen as constructive, and I completely agree with the author when he concludes that they are absolutely NOT constructive or rewarding in any way.

Let me add, from my personal experience as well as from the example of others around me, that over the years I have found nothing better and more worthwhile than becoming an active, and by that I mean working, member of our society immediately after graduating from school or university. Having a good job and thus contributing to the wealth and well-being of our country is infinitely more rewarding than drinking at some Thai beach!

I congratulate you on this article and hope you will keep drawing attention to the moral decline in our society, especially among young people, in the future.

Philip Arthur Philips
Bishop's Stortford, England

Time out: Spending a gap year abroad

• Don't use "Dear …".	Sir or Madam:
• Start by naming the article you refer to and giving the reason for writing your letter.	Having read your 6 September article "…", I would like to/I feel the need to point out … 1.
• State right away what you would like to praise/criticize about the article.	As a supporter of …, / 2. I totally agree / I see no reason why … 3.
• Present your arguments in a structured form. • Refer to the original article, but do not quote. • Go beyond the article to explain why you share/oppose the author's point of view.	4. What you need to keep in mind is … Your article raises the question whether … 5. The way I see it, … Although I understand why …, I cannot accept your overall conclusion that … I think you are mistaken if you believe … You overlook the fact that … You are absolutely right when you say that … 6. 7. 8.
• End your letter with a strong statement, e.g. a final appeal or a strong expression of your opinion.	9. Therefore, we should be careful … Consequently, I strongly support your view …
• Close the letter by writing your name and place of residence.	John Miller London, England

Checklist: Letter to the editor p. 133

B11 Write a letter to the editor in which you disagree with the way "gappers" are presented in the article.

You may think of your own experiences abroad or those of relatives and friends. Remember to refer back to points from the article that you feel very strongly about.

Here are some ideas to help you find arguments for your letter:
improving your language skills; personal development; good for your CV; …

1 Time out: Spending a gap year abroad

Getting to the point

Pre-reading

C1 Study the picture, the caption and the advice box on the left. Explain what kind of article you expect from these first impressions.

Owen Henry, 19, of Waterford, Va., graduated from high school last year. Now he's working on the *Lady Maryland*, a tall ship, as a deckhand[1] during his gap year in Baltimore. He'll enroll this fall at Oberlin College.

By Mike Buscher for USA TODAY

[1] deckhand = so. who works on a ship doing jobs such as cleaning

"Gap year" before college gives grads valuable life experience

by G. Jeffrey MacDonald, Special for USA TODAY

How to be productive

For a productive year between high school and college:
– **Secure a place in college first.** Then defer enrollment for a year. This is less hectic than spending the gap year doing applications.
– **Have a plan.** Set goals and create structure to prevent depressing
5 downtime at home.
– **Research programs.** If an organization can't recommend at least two alumni to discuss their experiences, don't sign up.
– **Respect your social needs.** The year represents a break with the crowd, so it's important to plan strategies for making new friends and
10 staying in touch with old ones.
– **Plan ahead for health insurance.** Some policies won't cover adult-age dependents if they cease to be full-time students. Check your policy several months in advance, then explore temporary insurance if necessary.
15 Source: Center for Interim Programs, Princeton, N.J.

Worn-out high school seniors are getting fresh encouragement from a range of sources to take a
20 break – a "gap year" – before plunging into college. But to be beneficial, it needs to involve more than rest
25 and relaxation.

Time out: Spending a gap year abroad

This spring, high schools in seven metropolitan areas hosted their first gap-year fairs to acquaint students with options for spending a year away from the academic treadmill. Earlier in the year, Princeton University announced plans to formalize a "bridge year" program for admitted students to do service work abroad before enrolling.

[...]

Though the concept may be new to many in the USA, it's an established tradition elsewhere. In the United Kingdom, for instance, about 11% of the 300,000 college-bound seniors take a gap year before enrolling. Australia puts up similar aggregate numbers in what's known Down Under as "going walkabout".

Reliable data for gap-year activity aren't available for the USA, but guidance counselors and college admissions officers say they're seeing a surge[2] of interest.

One contributing factor: The high-pressure senior year of high school increasingly leaves students drained and craving refreshment.

Also, counselors are coming to bless the gap-year option, and colleges increasingly are offering a deferred enrollment option as more and more "gappers" arrive on campus with enhanced focus, motivation and maturity — all of which bodes well[3] for their undergraduate years in college.

"Counselors are recognizing that there are many pathways to college," says David Hawkins, director of public policy and research at the National Association for College Admission Counseling. "They see that, if properly vetted, these opportunities could actually help students succeed in college."

[...]

Consultants agree gap years shouldn't be just "time off," and should instead be crafted with clear goals in mind.

But whether a gapper learns and grows more in a highly programmed environment than in one that's less predictable remains a topic open for discussion.

Some recommend adhering to a set of structured activities that minimize the likelihood of prolonged downtime at home or major pitfalls on the road.

"Most people need structure," says Holly Bull of the Center for Interim Programs. "Parents come to me halfway through a child's gap year and say, 'It's sort of falling apart here. We need more ideas or more structure.' So structure is important."

Others say that while the highly structured approach may be good for businesses that cater to gappers, too much "hand-holding" can hinder the maturation process that tends to happen in the absence of ample support systems.

"Unlike Europeans, (Americans') happiness to be handheld throughout the process creates demand for support services, orientation and premium products required to keep them safe and show them a good time," says Tom Griffiths, founder of gapyear.com. But "if you're not in a group, you get more out of it. It's just a fact that if you travel around the world on your own, you grow up."

Confidence from experience

U.S. gappers sing the praises of structured programs, but they also say they grew most when they had to live by their wits.

[...]

Owen Henry of Waterford, Va., opted in 2007 to take a gap year when he received a pile of college rejection letters. His goals for the year: to be challenged, gain work experience and clarify academic goals. He participated in a program for American gap-year students last fall at Oxford University, where he says he spent less than $10,000, and he decided on a career as an Arabic translator.

Since March, he has been handling two tons of sail as a deckhand on the Lady Maryland, a 104-foot-long tall ship and floating classroom in Baltimore. He gets room, board and $6.54 an hour. He has saved $1,600 of this for college, and he plans to enroll this fall at Oberlin College, to which he applied and was accepted during the gap year.

(Most experts recommend applying to colleges during senior year, getting accepted and then requesting a one-year deferral.)

"Feeling my hands cracking apart and being destroyed and slowly built up again with calluses[4]

---

[2] **surge** = a sudden increase in sth.
[3] **to bode well** = to be a sign that sth. good will happen
[4] **callus** = a hard thick area of skin caused by rubbing, especially on your hands and feet

was a slow and painful process," Henry says. But this was his first job, and he resolved, "I'm not quitting just because my hands are sore."

Learning from failure

[...]

Even mishaps can be a boon[5] by yielding[6] the very outcomes that a gap year is supposed to deliver.

Karl Haigler, author of The Gap Year Advantage: Helping Your Child Benefit From Time Off Before or During College, recalls a gapper who got malaria in Africa. "She had to cope, and she turned it into a positive. She said she learned to be an advocate because she had to advocate for herself to get health care."

Says Samer Hamadeh, co-founder of Vault.com, a career information company: "To be able to talk about a failure as an experience and how you learned from it — that's invaluable. So you can't go wrong. That's the bottom line. Just plan it, do it as a deferral (to college), have a goal and then go for it."

But figuring out how best to do a gap year is still a matter of balancing risks, potential benefits and personal interests.

In that mix, Bull says, students should do plenty of advance research and try to avoid potential nightmare situations, such as becoming ill without a solid support network in a developing country.

"You don't have to go through that as a parent or as a student," Bull says.

[5] **boon** = sth. useful that brings great benefits or makes your life easier
[6] **to yield** = to produce sth. useful

Comprehension

C2 Read the article published in 2008 and outline the reasons for the increase in the numbers of gappers and their experiences as described in the article.

Analysis

C3 Describe the author's attitude towards gap years and analyze the means he uses to support it.

Checklist: Text analysis p. 125

Comment

C4 A friend of yours has just returned from his/her gap year travelling around Thailand. Write a letter to the editor commenting on the views expressed in the article. Take into account what your friend has told you about his/her experiences.

To help you with your line of argumentation, look at the article in the B section again.

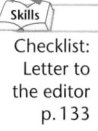
Checklist: Letter to the editor p. 133

Listening

D1 a) Card survey: In a listening comprehension, you may encounter a wide variety of texts (e.g. a lecture, an interview) and contexts (e.g. a radio show).
Note down further examples on cards.

b) Cluster your cards on the board. Group similar kinds of texts/contexts together.

c) There are a number of factors that might make understanding an audio or video clip difficult. Look at the cards on the board and explain when the following factors are relevant:

- background noise (e.g. traffic, people talking, etc.)
- slang
- English spoken by non-native speakers
- different varieties of English (e.g. regional accents, Australian English, South African English)
- poor pronunciation (e.g. incorrect/unclear pronunciation)
- talking too fast
- poor acoustic quality
- many different speakers, especially when speaking simultaneously

How to listen effectively
p. 152

D2 a) Usually, there are a lot of clues as to what an audio/audiovisual clip is about. Take a look at the following website and explain what helps you prepare for the listening/viewing comprehension that is to follow.

b) Having studied the website in detail, name topics that are likely to be covered in the programme.

Time out: Spending a gap year abroad

D3 Match the following aspects of a listening comprehension (1-7) with the tips on what you can do while listening (a-g).

1	topic-related keywords	a	Although you may think you recognize words and their meaning, it is always important that you do not rely only on guessing, but consider what fits the situation and the rest of what is said.
2	the intonation / emphasis	b	Listening for them will help you understand the general structure and notice the main topics of the listening text.
3	words you know from German or other foreign languages, sometimes also as English words that are now part of other languages, too	c	Knowing at least a part of an expression can often help you correctly guess what it means as a whole if you take the context into account.
4	the beginning / end / passages that lead over from one part to the next	d	They help you find out about the structure of the text and signal a new idea that may be relevant to your task.
5	the context	e	Some parts of a listening text are most likely to include a summary of the most important points that will be said or have already been said or at least give you some clues in that respect.
6	words / expressions that include English words you already know	f	As listening texts usually include a lot of unfamiliar words, this strategy may help you go beyond the English vocabulary you know.
7	structuring words (e.g. but/ however, before/after, in addition, in conclusion)	g	The words the speaker stresses may help you identify what is important to him and how he feels about the topic.

Time out: Spending a gap year abroad

How to listen effectively p. 152

D4 Watch a news clip about British gappers going to India.

www.diesterweg.de/cta/74014/links

a) Decide which of the following statements are true or false.

		true	false
1	India used to be a place where backpackers and hippies went.		
2	The number of gappers to India has risen because universities encourage more students to go abroad.		
3	18-year-old Nikki Dadhley did not get a place at university and decided to take a year out.		
4	She helps schoolchildren in Jaipur with their acting skills.		

b) Match the sentence halves. Note: There are more endings (a-f) than you need.

1	Richard Oliver believes that those students who do a gap year after school	a	are more aware of global problems.
2	Another advantage of students with gap-year experience is that they can take part in seminars better because they	b	are less likely to give up their university course because they start refreshed.
3	There are also many gappers like Oliver Harkus who	c	cannot find a job after university and hope to gain skills abroad and meet new people that can help them when they look for and find a job.
4	One of the reasons why people like Oliver Harkus go abroad is that they	d	want to start a new life with a new job in another country far away from Britain.
		e	are much better students than those who did not take a gap year.
		f	take a year out after finishing university.

c) Choose the correct answer.

1. According to Simon Ferrand, gap-year travellers do **not** face the danger of …

   a) drugs.
   b) aggressive sexual behaviour, especially towards girls.
   c) natural disasters.
   d) traffic accidents.

2. gogapyear.com …

   a) is a website about the activities of the Foreign Office abroad.
   b) tells you about school and universities abroad.
   c) gives you tips on how to sponsor your trip.
   d) provides you with information you need to prepare well for a gap year.

Time out: Spending a gap year abroad

1

DVD

Skills
How to listen effectively
p. 152

D5 a) Read the info-box below. Then listen to part of a lecture by Daniela Papi and outline her view on graduates doing volunteer work in no more than 150 words.

www.diesterweg.de/cta/74014/links

> **Info: Gappers and volunteer work**
>
> Many (young) people who decide to take a gap year after school or college simply travel around the world in order to have fun, see different places or take language classes, but others decide to do volunteer work while they are abroad. There are many organizations that take on gappers to help with their charities; often for board and lodging or a small amount of money. The most common occupation for gappers who do volunteer work is to teach at a school in a foreign country.

b) Listen again and list Papi's most important arguments against unprepared young people trying to work in charities in foreign countries. Then write a text in which you compare her arguments with the attitude the student in the e-mail below shows towards her volunteer work in Sri Lanka.

Listening and reading

D6 Imagine you are the friend who received the e-mail below. Answer your friend's email and comment on the attitude she shows towards her volunteer work. Take into consideration what you have learned from Papi's lecture, but also keep in mind that you are writing to a friend!

E-mail from volunteer in Sri Lanka:

To: l.jackson@ymail.com
Subject: Sri Lanka

Life in Sri Lanka seems to be getting better every week. Love working here, partly because the students are older so give me no sh*t and secondly because they all worship me, as I'm a volunteer, here to save them. So my mission to save the world is going quite well. The orphans are so cool, I was told one of the cutest boy's story, and
5 cried... his dad killed his mum by cutting her leg off then beating her in front of him and his 5 brothers and one sister. He is only 12 and this was 4 years ago. Love him. The boys at the orphanage are amazing. They don't understand yet what we're saying, so when we play Pictionary it's a little difficult.

Have decided to kidnap one of them, he's 8 and called Kalum, cutest boy ever in the
10 whole wide world. I adopted him when we had to go to the school sports day. Had to don a sari for the day, my, my, my, have never been so hot, maybe won't be doing that again in a hurry. It's awesome though! Everyone loved it that we made an effort, so we were the centre of attention, which was annoying as no one watched the sport, but we loved it!

2 Choices, choices, choices

Getting started

A1 a) Note down the countries you have already been to and why you went there. (e.g. holidays, school exchange, etc.)

b) Group work: Talk about where you have been, why you went there and how you experienced your stay(s) abroad.

c) Note down which country or countries you would like to go to in the future for:
- an internship
- a work and travel programme
- university studies
- a job

d) Milling around: Find someone in class who would like to go to the same country as you. Talk about your motivation to go to that particular country and what you would like to do there.

A2 a) Watch this video clip produced by Future Reach, an organisation which helps school-leavers. Find out what these young people did after leaving school.

www.diesterweg.de/cta/74014/links

b) Watch it again and note down:
- why they applied
- how they applied
- what they gained in experience
- why they would recommend it to others

A3 a) Read about the following opportunities for school-leavers abroad and collect words and phrases to describe the positive experiences they had.

Text 1	Text 2	Text 3	Text 4
- insight into a foreign country	- valued member of a team		

b) Pair work: Discuss
- which of the opportunities (if any) you would consider applying for and why.
- possible negative experiences you might encounter while studying or working abroad.

①
AuPair World – we connect • we care
Become an au pair and have the time of your life

Would you like to get an authentic insight into a foreign country? Experience another language and culture with the help of a host family? Make friends for life and improve your CV? Then why not become an au pair?

This is what Tatiana wrote about her experience as an au pair:
I went to the USA because I wanted to improve my language, travel, find new friends and, of course, experience American family life first hand. I expected the experience to be very different from any experiences I'd ever had before; and I truly was right about it!!!!! I loved every single part of it, even some negative moments I had can't make me look at it in a different way! It's probably because I was lucky to get the best host family ever!
www.aupair-world.net

Choices, choices, choices: Applying to work or study abroad

  2

Future Reach

"What struck me about the experience was the integration into a team in which I'm a genuinely valued member, and am given work to do that makes a real contribution to the work of my colleagues. There is no menial photocopying or making coffee. Instead I do work on a similar level to that of the analysts around me. The sense of responsibility I have outweighs what I was expecting and makes the job challenging but also a lot more satisfying. I highly recommend this programme; it provides a unique opportunity to get right into the heart of a hugely successful and competitive business world and can give you a real taste of what life is like working in the Investment Banking world."

3

Voluntary Service Abroad

I spent three amazing months teaching English to HIV positive children and vulnerable adults, whilst living with an Ethiopian family in a host home.

Every day was so ridiculously rewarding that the one hour up (and down) hill trek and challenging living and working conditions seemed trivial by the end. Seeing my students improve day on day is something I won't forget.

Aside from designated roles, which vary from teaching English to sports, volunteers were able to explore the wonderful culture of their temporary home. I can remember leaving, and how my sadness mixed with satisfaction; it is never easy leaving people, whom you have become attached to, but it is also never easy taking a chance and doing something you never dreamed you could.

It's an opportunity to experience another culture, challenge yourself and develop transferrable skills to bring back with you. The three months volunteering could be part of post-school or college skills development, or a career break.

You don't need cash, skills or qualifications to take part in VSO ICS [1] – just the ambition to make a difference.

[1] **VSO ICS** = Voluntary Service Abroad International Citizen Service

4

StudyAbroad

I chose to study abroad mainly because I wanted to meet new people, with the same interest as me – the desire to leave a familiar place. I've always loved learning about new cultures and exploring foreign areas, I love the jargon, food, and difference in lifestyle. Australia was perfect because they speak English and it's on the other side of the world. (…)

I think I really grew as a person and fully indulged in the Australian experience and culture. I'm laidback now, I've actually got 'no worries' all the time. And thanks to Australia – I'm brave and adventurous. This experience was more than I could have ever mapped it out to be – I had the best friends in the entire world, and a new country and culture to explore, which I certainly did. (…) And as cheesy as this next statement is going to be – I couldn't be more thankful for a whole world worth exploring.

Choices, choices, choices: Applying to work or study abroad

A4 a) Read the following text and say who it addresses.

b) List words and phrases used to describe the advantages of gaining work experience abroad.

Work experience and internships
Experience abroad

Find out about the benefits of jetting off to learn new skills and show potential employers that you're no run-of-the-mill candidate

The advantages of gaining work experience have been highlighted by employers and careers services alike for many years now, and those same values continue to work wonders for young people hoping to boost their employability and secure that coveted first job in their chosen industry.

However, there is a whole new breed of graduates who are able to further distinguish themselves from the crowd by gaining work experience abroad.

Benefits of work experience abroad
Some people might wonder if there's any point heading to a new country to gain experience. "All the skills I can gain from work experience in a foreign country I can gain here," they might say. "And what about the costs and logistics involved with moving abroad for months at a time?"

However, there is a whole host of benefits that these doubters seem to have failed to consider:

A5 You are the Careers Advisor at an English school. Prepare a talk to give to school-leavers motivating them to spend time abroad before they start their further education. Write and give the talk using the words and phrases you have collected in the A-section.

- **Culture and community** – working abroad shows your desire to get stuck in and work alongside local people, rather than stand back and take in the culture from afar while you drift through the country as a tourist.
- **Sink or swim** – demonstrate to potential employers that you can cope in a multicultural, multilingual working environment and produce great work in the process. Even if you go to work in an English-speaking country, employers will see that you can rise to the challenge and succeed despite being out of your comfort zone, away from your friends and family.
- **Language skills** – these are hugely valuable to employers and spending time abroad and working alongside non-English speakers will help them improve. Remember, though, that languages are most valuable alongside another specialism, so don't pin all your hopes of employment on your new-found linguistic finesse.
- **Get up and go** – moving abroad and finding work experience shows motivation, independence, maturity and adaptability - all extra ticks on your job application forms.
- **Travel** – this is usually a secondary motive for many people, but it is quite a nice bonus.

Your opportunities
Internships – whether paid or unpaid – are a fantastic way to secure overseas work experience, and can be arranged with the help of a range of third-party organisations.

In a competitive job market, you may well find that expanding your horizons and gaining work experience abroad will help you reap the rewards in your future career.

2 Choices, choices, choices: Applying to work or study abroad

Practice section

Reading and writing

B1 a) Pair work: Read the job description and talk about whether you would want to apply for this programme.

b) Read the job description again and note down which of the required skills you have at your disposal and which you are lacking.

[1] program (AmE) = programme (BrE)

http://www.sunvilresort.com/jobs/iwcp.html

Sunshine Village Resort

Job Title	International Work and Culture Program[1]
Job Description	Our International Work and Culture Program is a twelve-month program at Sunshine Village Resort, in Orange County, California. Participation in this program will give you the opportunity to share your country's culture, customs, and traditions with our guests from all around the world. Among other things, the program involves assisting guests with language difficulties, ticket and dining reservations and special needs as well as giving them general information about our theme parks.
Basic Qualifications	To be eligible to apply for the International Work and Culture Program, you MUST: • Speak English fluently • Be at least 18 years of age to apply • Be available to work Sunday through Saturday, including days and nights • Have experience in customer service and guest relations • Demonstrate strong computer proficiency • Have cash handling skills (foreign currencies, credit card transactions) • Demonstrate strong problem solving and decision-making skills • Show ability to manage conflict resolution • Be able to handle confidential information
Preferred Qualifications	Fluent in French, German, Japanese, Portuguese or Spanish
Industry	Leisure and Travel: Theme Park Destinations
Pay Rate	Successful applicants will earn an hourly rate of $10.75 per hour.
Additional Information	Applicants should submit a covering letter of not more than 300 words, and a CV to the following address: Mr Jonathan Rodriguez Personnel Manager Sunshine Kingdom Theme Parks 18700 Ward Street Fountain Valley CA 92708 US

Choices, choices, choices: Applying to work or study abroad

B2 a) Read the following covering letter from a young British school-leaver applying for admission to the programme. Decide which of the required skills he has/has not got.

b) Pair work: Discuss Daniel's chances of being accepted for the programme.

Your contact information	50, Windmill Drive, Newham, Staffordshire ST12 5TZ Tel: 02531 88706 Email: DanHaw@binternet.com
Employer contact information	Jonathan Rodriguez Personnel Manager Sunshine Kingdom Theme Parks 18700 Ward Street Fountain Valley CA 92708 US
Salutation	Dear Mr Rodriguez
Introduction: Information on the job you are applying for and why you are applying for it.	I am writing to apply for your International Work and Culture Program, as advertised on your website last week. Please find enclosed my CV. I am in my last year of school and wish to gain some experience working abroad before starting a university course in tourism and foreign languages next year. It would be a fantastic opportunity to work in one of the world's most famous Theme Parks and look after guests from all over the world.
Main part: Describe what you have to offer the employer, why you are qualified for the job and how your skills and experience are a match for the position you are applying for.	Having grown up and been educated in England, I speak English fluently. My mother, however, comes from Germany, and since I speak German with her and visit my relatives in Hamburg regularly, I can also claim to be fluent in German. I am a conscientious person, who works hard and learns quickly. I am quick to pick up new skills and eager to learn from others. Moreover, I thoroughly enjoy working in a team. I believe I could therefore fit easily into your program and successfully accomplish any of the jobs you choose to give me. Since I have no personal commitments, the working hours will not be a problem. Having regularly worked in a big department store at the weekend and during the school holidays, I have gained useful experience in handling cash and credit card transactions and generally working with customers. If necessary, I can provide a reference from my employer. Finally, I would like to add that I have a high level of computer competence and am proficient in MS Word, Excel and PowerPoint, since this is a general requirement for my A-level courses in Maths, IT and Social Studies.
Closing lines: Thank the employer for considering you for the position.	Thank you for taking time to consider my application. I look forward to hearing from you in the near future. Yours sincerely, Daniel Hawthorne

2 Choices, choices, choices: Applying to work or study abroad

B3 Daniel also submitted the following CV with his application. Read the CV and say what additional qualifications Daniel has for the job.

B4
a) Read the CV and the advice in the margin carefully.
b) Think of what kind of internship you would like to do.
c) Milling around: Find two or three other students who are looking for similar internships and decide which qualities and skills are required for such a job.
d) Write your CV applying for this internship.

Margin notes (left)	CV	Margin notes (right)
Name in large font to stand out.	**Daniel Hawthorne**	Address in neat space-saving form.
Email address and mobile number are the most convenient way for recruiters to contact you.	50, Windmill Drive, Newham, Staffordshire ST12 5TZ Mobile: 004478798321 Email: DanHaw@binternet.com	

EDUCATION
2008 – 2015   St Thomas' School, Newham

A Levels 2015
Maths   predicted grade A*
IT   predicted grade A
Social Studies   predicted grade B

GCSEs 2013
8 GCSE passes including Maths grade A, IT grade A and French and History grade B

2002 – 2008   Newham Primary School

(Right margin: CV in reverse chronological order – most recent and usually most important first.)

(Left margin: Focus on people skills developed in the job.)

WORK EXPERIENCE
2013 – 2014 Store assistant at John Dean's Department Store, Stafford, on Saturdays and in the school holidays.

Worked in a busy team, often under pressure. Provided a quality service to customers. During the holidays worked as a cashier in the food hall.

(Left margin: Interests focus on key qualities: a team-player; interest in other cultures and languages.)

INTERESTS
Sport: Enjoy many team sports, including hockey and cricket and also play tennis for the county team.
Travel: Have travelled to Germany and France regularly and enjoy meeting and spending time with young people abroad.

(Left margin: Language levels)

SKILLS
- **Computing:** ECDL[1] qualifications in MS Word, PowerPoint and Excel
- **Peer Mediation:** Took part in a peer mediation program in year 9. Trained to help others find a peaceful resolution to conflicts.
- **Languages:** Fluent German (C1-2[2]) and good conversational French (B2[3])

Referee details available on request

(Right margin: Simple but effective bullet points to underline key skills. Precise description of computer and language skills.)

---

[1] **ECDL** = European Computer Driving Licence
[2] **C1-2** = language level of Proficient User according to Common European Framework of Reference for Languages
[3] **B2** = Language Level of Independent User

Choices, choices, choices: Applying to work or study abroad

B5 Read the following advertisement and summarize in one sentence what kind of internship is being advertised.

 http://www.ml.com/jobs/internship/advert

Internship Programmes with Bank of America Merrill Lynch – Summer 2015
Applications for our summer 2015 paid pre-university internship opportunities are open now.

Internship opportunities in London & Chester
In 2015 we are running paid internship programmes in both London and Chester at Bank of America Merrill Lynch.

Who should apply?
Applicants should be exceptional individuals who meet our rigorous criteria, which include a good academic record, sound analytical skills including an aptitude for numbers together with evidence of great teamwork skills at school or in extra-curricular activities.

Our pre-university internships programmes are a rare opportunity to experience actual working life within a top graduate employer before you start your university studies. They are designed to help our clients identify talent for the future. So we want to hear from candidates who have an interest in and are open to a career within the investment or corporate bank divisions.

Students must be planning to attend university in 2015 or 2016 (if a gap year is planned). Maths A-level is a requirement. We have summarized additional characteristics that we are looking for below:

- Team work
- Leadership qualities
- Interpersonal skills
- Willingness to learn
- Drive and initiative
- Business awareness

How do I apply?
Send us your CV and a covering letter explaining why you are applying for the internship and what qualifies you for it. The deadline for receipt of completed applications is 9:00 a.m. on Monday 13th January 2015.

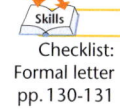
Checklist: Formal letter pp. 130-131

B6 Read the advert again and compare it with the one in B1 and explain how they differ.

B7 Write a covering letter applying for the internship advertised in B5.

Checklist
Covering letter
- ✓ Observe the rules for formal letter writing: salutation, layout etc.
- ✓ Include information on where you may be contacted.
- ✓ Refer to the post you are applying for and why you are applying for it in the first paragraph.
- ✓ In the main part describe any of your qualifications and skills that are relevant to the post.
- ✓ In the last part of the letter thank the recipient for considering your application.
- ✓ Check spelling and grammar carefully.

Language support
I am writing to apply for ..., as advertised in ...

I am a conscientious person, who ...
I enjoy working in a team.
I have gained useful experience in ...

I will be glad to supply you with any further information required.
I have attached/ enclosed the following documents: CV, references.

2 Choices, choices, choices: Applying to work or study abroad

Getting to the point

Pre-speaking

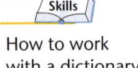
How to work with a dictionary pp. 142-143

C1 a) Write down three jobs that you might take on in the future. Use a dictionary to find out the English expressions for them if you do not already know it. Write each job on a separate piece of paper.

b) Cluster the jobs on the board in a word web and copy it.

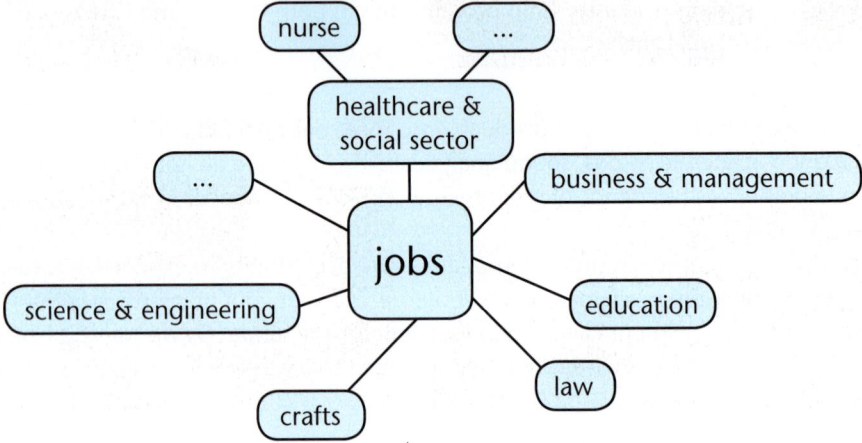

c) Think-pair-share: Note down what benefits and challenges jobs may have.

benefits	challenges
to have your own office	to fulfill the company's expectations (e.g. higher sales, new customers)
...	...

Speaking: Monologue

How to improve your oral skills pp. 148-149

How to give feedback/peer-edit pp. 144-145

C2 a) Choose two photos – one illustrating a job that you find attractive and one showing a job that does not appeal to you so much.

b) Group work (4): Take turns to present the two photos chosen in a) by:
- describing what kind of jobs they illustrate and
- explaining why you like/dislike those jobs.

The others listen to give feedback on the presentation afterwards. The checklist may help you.

> **Checklist**
> *Giving feedback/Peer-edit*
> ✓ Was the presentation easy to follow (correct pronunciation, pauses where necessary, emphasis on important points, clear structure, correct use of language)?
> ✓ Did he/she use different and suitable words to describe the photo?
> ✓ Did he/she present his/her material confidently and competently?

Choices, choices, choices: Applying to work or study abroad

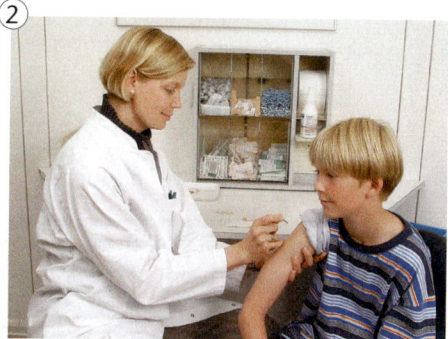

Language support: describing a photo
In the photo/on the left/right, you can see …
In the foreground/background, there is/are …
The clothes, namely … to be precise, are typical of …
… is busy with a typical activity – …
… is displaying typical behaviour of a … as he/she …

2 Choices, choices, choices: Applying to work or study abroad

C3 a) Group work (4): Each member of the group focuses on one of the photos below. Take turns to present your photos to the rest of the group while the others take notes to give feedback. For your presentations consider these two tasks:

- Describe which challenging situation at the workplace is depicted in your photo.
- Speculate on possible reasons for it as well as any consequences it may have.

b) Give feedback to each other.

Skills
How to give feedback/peer-edit
pp. 144-145

Pre-speaking

C4 a) Think-pair-share: If you apply for a job in another country, it is often not possible for a company to meet applicants in person. Therefore more and more job interviews are done online with the help of video conferencing programmes such as Skype.

Note down ideas of what you should keep in mind when you prepare for such an interview.

b) Watch the following video and note down tips about how you should prepare for a Skype interview. Compare them to your original list in a).

www.diesterweg.de/cta/74014/links

c) Read the article below and add further points to your list of tips.

Top tips for Skype interviews

From inappropriate posters in the background to sipping on a beer, Skype interviews can make jobseekers either feel even more nervous than usual or as though they're off the hook[1]. And they're on the rise[2]. 18% of candidates have experienced a video interview in the past year, more than double the amount from a year ago, according to a survey by Right Management. 82% of hiring managers have used Skype, and 6% have used pre-recorded platforms.

[1] **to be off the hook** = *(infml)* to feel like a situation is not as unpleasant as expected
[2] **to be on the rise** = to be increasing

Although people are used to being on video to family and friends, with a potential employer on the other end there are a few things you need to think about:

Preparation is key

You're in control of what shows on the screen so make sure you set the scene ahead of time, considering the right lighting and surroundings. Tracy Johnson, founder of Brainbox Consulting, says: "Be aware of what is on the wall behind you. Tatty posters and an unmade bed won't make the best impression. Check out the alignment of your camera and screen too – you may not actually be making eye contact with the interviewer and this can interfere with developing that all-important connection."

As for a regular interview, you also need to think about what to wear. You'll only be seen from the waist up, so you might be tempted to dress down, but this can be a risky strategy.

"Your interviewer will only find out that you're in your pyjamas if you have to stand up to get something, so strictly speaking you can wear what you like. However, being in business dress might make you feel the part and help with your performance," says Joanna Keilt, consultant at Futureboard.

You may also want to think about doing a mock interview to see if you need to adapt your style for technology. Mike Higgins, career coach at This is My Path, says: "If you can, do a dry run with a friend or someone who is a regular interviewer. If you are feeling brave, you can even record it and play back later. Pick out two things that you would like to improve for next time."

Have a plan B

While there's no worry you'll be held up by a late train, or get lost finding the right building, there is always the potential for technical issues. Make sure you know who is making the call and sign in early. Keilt says: "Download Skype well in advance of the interview and make sure you have a practice call to a friend to iron out any issues. Also, where possible, use headphones and a microphone to conduct the interview: this helps prevent feedback. If you can't hear your interviewer, let them know so they can try to fix the problem."

Honesty is the best policy if you have issues[3]. If you can't sort it out, suggest rearranging the call or using a phone for the audio, and Skype for the video.

During the interview

Something you may not have thought about is social interaction and how your body language comes across on camera. A Skype interview gives you less time to make a positive impression, says Tracy Johnson.

"You need to develop a rapport with the interviewer as quickly as possible. Think about your non-verbal communication: make lots of eye contact, smile and sit up straight. Roll your shoulders back and down so that you have good posture, open your chest and speak clearly." Mike Higgins agrees: "With audio and video channels, less body language information is transmitted, so focus on matching the tone and pace of your voice to the message you are trying to convey. If you say you are excited about a project, sound excited. If there is a mismatch between tone and message, the interviewer will go with the former rather than the latter."

If you can't Skype at home

If you don't have the right technology for the interview at home, you need to think carefully about where to do it. "If you don't have Skype at home, then ask your university or college careers service if they have a room that you can use – some will offer you a room for a telephone interview too," says Tracy Johnson.

"If you have to interview in a public place, let your interviewer know in advance, says Joanna Keilt. "Arranging an interview outside of lunchtime hours should mean that the coffee shop or café is less crowded. Avoid main roads at all costs."

[3] **to have issues** = to have problems that need solving

Choices, choices, choices: Applying to work or study abroad

C5 Pair work: No matter if the interview is done via Skype or in person, you need to be prepared. Watch the video and complete the grid below. One of you concentrates on what you shouldn't do, the other one on what you should do. Later complete the grid by telling each other what you have noted down.

www.diesterweg.de/cta/74014/links

Aspect of the interview	What you shouldn't do	What you should do
Clothes and make-up		
Handshake		
How to answer some key questions		
Other dos and don'ts		

Speaking: Dialogue

C6 Pair work: You work on this page, your partner goes to page 36.

(A)
You find examples of typical job interview questions below.

a) Read out your first question. Your partner should answer it as well as he/she can. You compare it to the professional tips given. Tell your partner what he/she did right and how he/she could improve his/her answer.

b) Now your partner reads out his/her first question for you and does the same. Then you take turns until you have covered all the questions.

c) Note down the most important advice for each question.

Q1: What is your greatest weakness?

A1:
You should be careful when you answer this question. First of all, your answer should not include anything that is highly important to the position you are applying for.
If the job requires you to get in touch with a lot of different people, it is not a good idea to say that you feel uncomfortable around people you do not know. You should therefore choose something that is not directly relevant to the main duties of your job.
It is also a good idea to be very specific in order to limit your weakness to something that can be clearly defined and that you could improve on. For example, you may sometimes find it difficult to react very spontaneously in situations you are not used to. This is better than saying that you are not spontaneous or flexible, which may be necessary in your job. You could instead add that with experience you have no problem with quick reactions and decisions or you could say that you are working on the problem, but that you prefer detailed and careful planning, which is positive, and this is something that makes spontaneous decisions difficult.

Q3: How would you describe yourself?

A3:
When answering this question, you should keep in mind what kind of job in what kind of company you are applying for. If your job involves a lot of teamwork and social interaction, you could say something like this: "I'm a people person. I really enjoy meeting and working with a lot of different people." But you shouldn't say anything that doesn't fit your real character.

Q5: What are your hobbies?

A5:
Not all the questions in an interview will be just about the position at hand. The interviewer will try to get a better idea of who you are as a person in general. So be prepared to talk about your free-time activities or hobbies. What you should avoid at all cost are answers that involve partying, gambling, hanging out and other activities that might be considered superficial or even illegal. Sports activities can demonstrate health and fitness. Volunteer work shows that you are willing to put in extra work for others, are socially-minded and are willing to take over responsibility even if it may not be a "fun" activity at first glance. If you do any activities that broaden your mind (e.g. evening classes in another foreign language) or are considered a sign of a varied education (e.g. playing an instrument), you should definitely include those. All in all, it is always good to mix different kinds of activities so that you come across as a person with many interests and skills.

Q7: Describe a difficult work situation and how you overcame it.

A7:
You should give a specific example and say what you did to solve the problem. You should avoid moaning about other people's mistakes, but rather respond positively even if someone else caused the mess you had to cope with, e.g. by saying something like "Even though it was difficult when one of my fellow students no longer took part in the project, I knew that this would not stop me from finishing it in the best possible way – even if it meant a lot of extra hours."

(B)
You find examples of typical job interview questions below.

a) Read out your first question. Your partner should answer it as well as he/she can. You compare it to the professional tips given. Tell your partner what he/she did right and how he/she could improve his/her answer.

b) Now your partner reads out his/her first question for you and does the same. Then you take turns until you have covered all the questions.

c) Note down the most important advice for each question.

Q2: What is your greatest strength?

A2:
This is one of the easier questions. You should refer to the personal qualities, skills and experience that are directly related to what is required by the job. If your job is about being with other people, e.g. charity work, working as an aupair, etc., you should emphasize social activities in which you have taken over responsibility such as coaching a children's football team, being in the scouts or a religious youth group, etc.

Q4: How do you handle stress and pressure?

A4:
Stress is part of basically any job, so it should become clear that you can cope with stress. However, you should say something more substantial than just "I can cope with stress". You could reply in one of the following ways, for example: "I actually work better under pressure and I really enjoy taking on a challenge." You can also acknowledge stress, but express that you know how to deal with it, e.g. by saying something like this: "I know that this kind of work can be stressful, but I have developed ways to reduce stress. When I go to the gym or jogging, I can reduce the stress that has built up over time."

Q6: What motivates you?

A6:
There is no right or wrong answer here, but you should make it clear what motivates you in the context of school and work and share your enthusiasm. It should be clear that it is not just fun you are after, but making customers happy, for example, or doing your job as well as you can, etc.

Q8: What do people most often criticize about you?

A8:
This question should be answered very carefully as it aims at finding out how sensitive you are and how you cope with criticism. You should avoid appearing "too perfect", but at the same time you should not create the impression that others criticize you in a school or work context. You may choose an example from your free time, something that might also be interpreted positively at the same time or refer to something you were criticized for in the past, but have – since then – been able to improve on. Some examples could be "Some people sometimes think I'm too much of a perfectionist, but I always aim high and expect a lot from myself." or "Some time ago someone told me that I sometimes sounded too critical of other people's work. I took it to heart and now I have learnt to give only positive and supportive feedback."

Choices, choices, choices: Applying to work or study abroad

C7 a) Compare the scripts of the following passages from job interviews. Explain why interview B felt probably more rewarding and helpful for both the interviewer and the interviewee.

b) Read the interviews again and start a grid of useful phrases that you could use to make the interview run more smoothly – both as an interviewer and interviewee.

Interview A

Interviewer: Good afternoon. I'm Alexandra Thorpe and this is my colleague, Mr Patrick Tarbuck. I'm glad that you have followed our invitation and were able to come and see us here in person. I hope you've had no problem finding your way here.

James: No, it wasn't a problem.

Interviewer: To start with, I'd like you to tell us a little bit about yourself.

James: My name is James Carpenter. I'm 18 years old and I'm about to finish school this summer and I would like to gain some experience in your company as I'd like to study Business and Marketing from autumn this year.

Interviewer: Have you ever worked in a company before?

James: No, I haven't.

Interviewer: Why have you chosen to apply for an internship at our company?

James: You are an internationally active company, which is very interesting to me as I would like to combine my Business Studies with my foreign language skills.

Interviewer: Please tell me a little bit more about what you do in your free time.

James: I have been very busy preparing for my A-levels lately, but I like to do some sports to reduce my stress level and keep fit.

Interview B

Interviewer: Good afternoon, I'm Robert Markham. Thank you for coming to this interview at such short notice. As I said in my email I'm on a business trip next week, so I thought it might be more convenient for you to come in before that. I hope it didn't mean too much hassle for you.

Francesca: No, not at all. Actually, it was even more convenient for me to come today as the final exams are coming up and I'm much more flexible this week. Thank you for inviting me anyway.

Interviewer: You sent in a very interesting application for an internship, so I'd like to find out a little bit more about you in person. Although I've got your application in front of me, it would be great if you could start by saying concisely again what made you apply for an internship at our company.

Francesca: As I already pointed out in my application, there are basically two reasons why I would like to be accepted for an internship here at Markham & Partners. First of all, I'm planning to start studying Law in autumn and your company is one – if not the – most renowned law firm in the business. So I thought it would be a great opportunity to gain more insight into the practical side of working in this field so that I can see the reasoning behind some of the coursework we'll have to do. Secondly, I know that you are a large law firm that has an excellent reputation with lawyers that specialize in a wide variety of fields. I don't know if it is possible, but I would really like to get to know different departments.

Interviewer: You're right that we are one of the biggest firms in the business and

Choices, choices, choices: Applying to work or study abroad

> hopefully also one of the best – that's our aim at least. Coming back to your wish to get to know different departments, I would assign you to one department to one of our junior members of staff so that you have someone at your side who can look after you. This person would know what a Law course at university looks like so you would be able to ask him or her about that as well. But we can definitely arrange a tour of the company and you may be able to talk to the members of staff.
>
> **Francesca:** That sounds fantastic, even better than what I was hoping for. But I wouldn't like to be a burden on your staff anyway.
>
> **Interviewer:** Don't worry. In order to make the most of your time, however, I'd like to know what kind of IT skills or other possibly relevant skills you may have.
>
> **Francesca:** As I have already written in my CV, I'm familiar with all the major MS Office programs. I also did a course in typing, so I hope I could be of help in that respect as well. Other than that, you'd have to be more specific. Maybe there are other skills that might be useful to you.
>
> **Interviewer:** No, that was exactly what I was hoping for.

C8 a) Pair work: Choose one of the job adverts on pages 39-41. Flip a coin to decide who takes over the role of the interviewer and who the interviewee. Read the job advert carefully and prepare for the job interview.

b) Group work (4): The interviewer starts with the interview. Imagine it is a Skype interview.

Another pair (pair B) watches you and takes notes to give feedback. Then pair B presents their first Skype interview and receives feedback from pair A afterwards.

c) Pair work: Choose another job advert. Now switch roles. Read the job advert and prepare for the interview.

d) Group work (4): Follow the same steps as in b).

Skills
How to give feedback/peer-edit
pp. 144-145

Checklist
Giving feedback
✓ Was the dialogue easy to follow (correct pronunciation, pauses where necessary, emphasis on important points, clear structure, correct use of language)?
✓ Did they explain clearly what they wanted to ask/answer about the job in question and the necessary qualifications?
✓ Did they interact and refer to each other's points?

Choices, choices, choices: Applying to work or study abroad

Looking for a live-in au pair in Hammersmith/Brook Green area (W6)
Brook Green, London

We are a Scottish/Australian family living in Hammersmith/Brook Green (W6) with two children – Robbie (6) and Annabel (4). Both my husband and I work full time – my husband works in the city and I run my business from home. We have had a wonderful au pair live with us for the last two years who is now ready to move on and pursue a different career. We are therefore looking for a "live-in" au pair to join our family in August/September for approximately 12 months.

In summary, you will be responsible for all of the children's day-to-day activities as well as some aspects of running the home. Approximately 7.15 am - 10 am and then 3.30 pm - 7 pm during term time and full time over school holidays.

- Overseeing children's breakfast and assisting with getting them ready for school
- Walking them to school (10 min walk away)
- Picking them up from school
- Supervizing relevant after-school activities
- Preparing after school snacks
- Preparing children's dinner
- Assisting with children's homework
- Overseeing children's bath time and getting them ready for bed
- Weekly changing of their bed linen – washing and changing
- Regular washing their clothes and preparing school uniform
- Helping keep their bedroom tidy
- Help monitor their progress at school and with their friends – being our "eyes and ears" when we are unable to see what goes on at play-dates etc.

We are looking for someone who is bright, energetic and thoroughly enjoys engaging with children. Qualities you will need:

- Extremely patient and understanding of our children's needs
- Excellent English
- Extremely organized and able to multi-task – such as overseeing homework, getting dinner ready, running bath and preparing school uniform for the next day
- Adaptable
- Positive and happy
- Very safety-conscious
- Happy to "roll up sleeves[1]" and help around the house – help with day-to-day house/kitchen tidying such as unloading dishwasher, sorting out kids toys etc. (we have a cleaning lady once a week for heavy duty cleaning and ironing).

Essential experience
- At least 3 years of experience working with young school age children
- First Aid Certificate
- Non-smoker
- Ideally experience teaching in a nursery or school

If you are interested, please email a copy of your CV, a letter explaining a little about who you are and your experience, a photograph, when you are able to start, and an outline of what you would like to be paid.

[1] to roll up o's sleeves = *here*: to get involved with sth.

Delta Summer Sports Camp

Sports & Activity Ranger Job Details

Our Sports Activity Rangers are responsible for ensuring our 5-13 year olds have the holiday of a lifetime. Our Rangers work on seasonal contracts, working from June to September, throughout our high season! This role is for those who want to do a job they love in luxurious locations.

Our Rangers have to be able to think on their feet, organizing fun and varied activity programmes both on and off site.

Our vacancies are more suited to those who have worked as a sports coach or activity leader previously, however we also consider applications from experienced professionals looking for a change from the 9-5![1]

Essential Requirements
- Experience working with children aged 5-13 in a sports coaching/activity environment
- Sports Coaching or Activity leadership qualifications
- Ability to work in a team
- Knowledge of safety procedures
- Full, clean, driving license

Essential Attributes
- Passion for working with children
- Team player
- Outgoing nature
- Professional demeanour[2]
- Strong swimmer
- Creativity
- Positive attitude

Benefits
- Full training
- Return travel to/from the UK
- Accommodation
- Competitive salary
- Insurance
- Access to a company vehicle (location specific)

About us
Delta is a specialist provider for the sports and childcare sector.
We have vacancies in activity camps both in the UK and abroad. We're looking for the best people who stand out from the crowd, love working with children and want an amazing experience.

If you think you have what it takes to join our amazing team, complete your online profile today and email it to workabroad@deltasummer.com

---

[1] **9-5** = 9 am - 5 pm, the average working day in the UK
[2] **demeanour** /dɪˈmiːnə/ = the way someone looks and behaves

Sussex Serengeti Safari Park

This is an exciting opportunity for the right candidates to join the team at one of the UK's top safari parks for the 2015 season. The key to your success will be your ability to demonstrate first-rate customer service and become an outstanding ambassador for Sussex Serengeti Safari Park.

If you are committed to working as part of a team, in a fun environment, then we would like you to apply. Our aim is to ensure that everyone of our visitors has a day to remember and with your help we can achieve that. Candidates will be required to attend an Assessment Centre.

Assessment Centres tend to last no longer than four hours and we will require you to take part in a number of group activities which you will be expected to participate in whilst being observed and marked against the competencies/criteria for your particular role. The dress code is smart i.e. shirt and trousers/skirt (no jeans, trainers, sportswear, plimsolls or UGG style footwear).

Bank Holiday working is necessary due to the nature of our business and your own transport would be an advantage in view of our location.

Food & Beverage Unit Leader
We have a great opportunity for a Food & Beverage enthusiast to get stuck in to their next challenge supporting the Food & Beverage operation. We are recruiting unit leaders for a number of food outlets around the park to support the management team in achieving targets including revenue, guest experience and food safety.

Supporting your assistant manager you will work on the ground managing the daily operation of the unit and ensuring your team can deliver a first class service to all our guests so supervisory skills will be needed.

This position is on a fixed term contract working 5 days out of 7 based on 45 hours a week. Flexibility is required to meet the needs of the business and shifts will include weekends, early evenings and bank holidays.

If you have at least one year's experience in the food service industry and think you are suitable for this role, please forward your CV and covering letter detailing why to: recruitment@sussexserengeti.co.uk

Choices, choices, choices: Applying to work or study abroad

Mediation

Expressing the gist

D1 When working on a mediation task, you are not expected to translate the German text literally, but to express the content in your own English words.
First, you need to look closely at the task in order to identify the following three points that tell you what you have to do:

1. Who is the addressee and what is the situational context into which the mediation task is integrated?
2. What type of text should be produced?
3. What aspects of the content should you focus on or what purpose should your text serve?

a) Identify the elements in 1-3 above for each of the following mediation tasks:

A Kyle, ein ehemaliger US-amerikanischer Austauschschüler an Ihrer Schule, möchte nach seinem High-School-Abschluss gern in Deutschland studieren. Bei seinen Recherchen ist er auf den Begriff "duales Studium" gestoßen. In seiner E-Mail bittet er Sie nun um weitere Informationen dazu, damit er weiß, was genau darunter zu verstehen ist und welche Vor- und Nachteile ein solcher Studiengang bietet. Schreiben Sie ihm auf der Grundlage des folgenden Artikels eine Antwortmail, in der Sie Kyles Fragen beantworten.

B Als Teilnehmer an einer internationalen Jugendbegegnung zum Thema "Jugendarbeitslosigkeit" setzen Sie sich zusammen mit Gästen aus ganz Europa mit den Problemen Jugendlicher in Europa und den unterschiedlichen Lösungsansätzen auseinander. Zum Einstieg stellen alle Teilnehmer die Situation in ihrem Heimatland vor und fassen die wichtigsten Punkte in einem Artikel für die Veranstaltungswebseite zusammen.
Verfassen Sie einen solchen informierenden Artikel, in dem Sie die wichtigsten Informationen zu Ausbildung und Berufsperspektiven junger Deutscher auf der Grundlage des folgenden Zeitungsartikels vermitteln.

C Sie absolvieren ein Auslandspraktikum in der irischen Partnerfirma eines örtlichen Unternehmens. Als erster Teilnehmer an dem Programm für Schülerpraktikanten stellen Sie in einem kurzen Artikel für das firmeneigene Intranet Ihren neuen Kolleginnen und Kollegen das Konzept eines Schülerpraktikums und dessen wachsende Popularität in Deutschland auf der Grundlage des folgenden Zeitungsartikels vor.

Choices, choices, choices: Applying to work or study abroad

b) The points you considered in a) also have an impact on the kind of language and register you should use. For each example decide which register and kind of language is most suitable according to the task. The ideas below may help you.

> objective and matter-of-fact style – rhetorical devices – use of imagery – complex sentences – personal view – colloquial expressions – incomplete sentences – technical terms – slang – formal expressions – heading

c) Compare your results in class.

D2 a) The beginning of the article on page 44 from the *Berliner Zeitung* is the basis for working on task A (see D1). Read the beginning of the article and decide which text (1, 2 or 3) fits task A best.

- Give reasons for your choice.
- Explain what may still be good in the other versions.

(1)
Hi Kyle,
Great to hear from you again. It's been quite some time since you left and went back to the US. So it sounds really exciting and super cool that you'd like to come back. *Duales Studium* – well, I wouldn't do it, but here's what it's all about. You apply for such a position at a company. If you are lucky, they pick you and send you to uni. But when you're not at uni, you have to slave away in the company. OK, you get some cash for it, but no free time??? It takes three years all in all and afterwards your chances of getting a job at the company are quite good.

(2)
Hi Kyle,
It's great to hear that you would like to come back to Germany for your studies. You asked me what a *Duales Studium* is. It is an increasingly popular form of a three-year degree course at university. But as the word *dual* suggests, you do not only spend time at a university, but somewhere else as well, meaning a company which has selected you in an application process and pays for your studies, but expects you to work for them when you are not attending classes. This can make it quite stressful, but you are paid a salary as well and usually stand good chances of being offered a job after your graduation. That's why more and more school-leavers do it. Furthermore, those who choose this kind of a course like the combination of theory and its direct practical application at the company.

(3)
Dear Kyle,
I was delighted to hear from you after such a long time. I hope I can help you with your query. A *Duales Studium* is a kind of programme offered by many companies in cooperation with nearby universities. During the three years of the programme, you study both at a university and work for the company when there are no lectures. This means that a programme like this requires a lot of dedication and ability to cope with stress. However, your hard work is compensated for by the fact that the company covers your university fees and pays you a salary. Your employment guarantees that you may apply your newly-gained theoretical knowledge in practice. Eventually, you stand a good chance of being offered a permanent post after your graduation.

Berliner Zeitung

DUALES STUDIUM   Karriere – 24.02.2014

Kein Privatleben, aber sehr gute Aussichten

Lernen, lernen, lernen: Auch an der Hochschule für Technik und Wirtschaft Berlin kann man dual studieren.

von Barbara Weitzel

Im Unternehmen arbeiten und gleichzeitig die Hörsaalbank drücken: Ein duales Studium ist anstrengend, ermöglicht eine schnelle Karriere – und ist nicht für jeden das Richtige.

Hanna Langen weiß genau, wie es nach dem Abitur weitergehen soll, und sie nimmt dafür einiges auf sich. Die 19-Jährige steckt mitten in den Prüfungen, das Lernpensum ist enorm, schließlich soll es ein richtig guter Abschluss werden. Den braucht sie, denn Langen will gleich danach ein duales Studium beginnen. Ihr Ziel: ein Bachelor in International Business, also einer Kombination aus Betriebs- (BWL) und Volkswirtschaftslehre (VWL) auf internationaler Ebene an der Dualen Hochschule in Mannheim, dazu die Ausbildung bei der Gesellschaft für Internationale Zusammenarbeit (GIZ) oder bei einem Pharmaunternehmen wie Fresenius oder Pfizer. Hanna Langen würde drei Jahre lang abwechselnd die Hochschulbank drücken und arbeiten, so sieht es das duale Studium vor. Das Unternehmen zahlt die Studiengebühren und ein Gehalt. Der Student bekommt Theorie und Praxis im Doppelpack – und sehr wahrscheinlich einen gut bezahlten Job im Anschluss.

LOHNENDE DISZIPLIN

Doch das duale Studium hat seinen Preis, schon bevor man es begonnen hat. Langen schreibt neben dem Lernen Bewerbungen, informiert sich, führt Gespräche, und einen Besuch im Assessment-Center – der klassische Weg der beteiligten Firmen, die Begabtesten und Belastbarsten herauszufiltern – hat die Abiturientin auch schon hinter sich. „Neun Stunden lang, mit den Besten der Besten, danach war ich fix und fertig", erzählt sie. Lohnt sich der Stress? Was steckt hinter der begehrten Berufsausbildung, warum wollen das so viele junge Leute? „Ein duales Studium ist viel spannender und erlebnisreicher als ein normales, eher trockenes Lernstudium", sagt Langen. „Da kann man das erlernte theoretische Wissen direkt in der Praxis anwenden. Das erleichtert auch den Berufseinstieg nach dem Studium."

Viele sehen das so. Die Zahl der dualen Studenten steigt Jahr für Jahr, die der angebotenen Studiengänge und der ausbildenden Unternehmen ebenso. Die Datenbank Ausbildung Plus des Bundesinstituts für Berufsbildung (BIBB) verzeichnet für das Jahr 2012 64.000 junge Erwachsene, die an einer (Fach-)Hochschule oder einer Berufsakademie studierten und nebenbei in einem Unternehmen lernten. Das sind 7,5 Prozent mehr als im Vorjahr. Tendenz: steigend.

Choices, choices, choices: Applying to work or study abroad

D3 Sometimes it is not easy to find suitable English words for German phrases and expressions used in the original text. This may be for two reasons:

1. It is an idiomatic expression which cannot be translated literally into English, e.g. *Die Diskussion dreht sich im Kreis.* – There is no one or nothing that is actually spinning around.

2. It is a concept that cannot be translated adequately into English because it can only be fully understood if you know about German culture. *Gymnasium* for example is a type of school that does not exist in Britain or the US – it is best to explain it instead of looking for an inadequate translation: "… went to a *Gymnasium*, i.e. a type of school aiming at the more able pupils and preparing for university studies …"

Write down English words/phrases/paraphrases for the following German expressions from the article above:

1. die Hörsaalbank drücken
2. Abitur
3. im Doppelpack bekommen
4. seinen Preis haben
5. fix und fertig sein

D4 a) Now read the complete article from *the Berliner Zeitung* (pages 44 and 46-47) carefully and note down relevant information that you need to write the email to Kyle (see task D1a).

b) Use your notes to write your mediation text.

> **Checklist**
> ✓ Concentrate on relevant details that are required by the task.
> ✓ Use a register and style that is appropriate to the addressee(s) and the situation described in the task.
> ✓ Use indirect speech if necessary.
> ✓ Explain the cultural background of German terms if necessary.
> ✓ Do not translate word for word.
> ✓ Do not follow the structure of the original text. Rearrange the information as you need it to fulfil the task.
> ✓ Do not add any information.
> ✓ Leave out your own opinion.

Ebenfalls wachsend ist die Zahl der Studiengänge, 910 verschiedene waren es 2012 für die Erstausbildung, dazu kamen 474 Studiengänge für die Weiterbildung. Die meisten dualen Studiengänge gibt es in den betriebswirtschaftlichen Fächern, aber auch die Kooperationen zwischen Unternehmen und Hochschulen im ingenieurwissenschaftlichen Sektor sind enorm gestiegen. Langsamer, aber ebenfalls stetig wächst der Markt im Bereich Sozialwesen, also Studiengänge in der Pflege, der Rehabilitation und in Sozialer Arbeit.

KEINE ZEIT ZUM JOBBEN

Die Vorteile eines dualen Studiums liegen auf der Hand: Neben der bereits genannten Praxisnähe knüpfen die Berufsanfänger wertvolle Kontakte, in der Regel werden sie nach dem Studium vom Unternehmen übernommen. Außerdem verdienen sie Geld und bekommen die Studiengebühren bezahlt. Für Hanna Langen ein starker Grund bei einem Studium, neben dem keine Zeit zum Jobben bleibt: „Man ist etwas unabhängiger von den Eltern", sagt sie.

Der 19-Jährigen ist klar, dass man für diese Vorteile einen Preis zahlen muss: Viel Stress komme auf sie zu, und viel Disziplin müsse sie aufbringen, sagt Langen, und: „Freizeit hat man auch nicht viel in den drei Ausbildungsjahren." Nicht viel Freizeit? Keine, wenn man Torsten Licht fragt: „Auf Privatleben muss man in dieser Zeit verzichten", sagt der Absolvent im Studiengang Logistic Management. Die drei Jahre, in denen er an der Hamburg School of Business Administration studierte und die Praxismonate in einem Logistik-Konzern absolvierte, seien knallhart gewesen. Die Wechsel zwischen Unternehmen und Uni machte er mal alle drei Monate, manchmal aber auch alle drei Wochen. 14 Klausuren in 10 Tagen waren normal, und an den Wochenenden bereitete er sich auf die Kaufmannsgehilfenprüfung zum Schifffahrtskaufmann vor. „Ein akademisches Studium ist das nicht. Man prügelt sich den Stoff in den Kopf und hat vieles nach der Prüfung gleich wieder vergessen", sagt Torsten Licht. „Wer richtig studieren will, soll lieber einen klassischen Abschluss wählen."

Das duale Studium sei genau das Richtige für Leute, die möglichst schnell in einem Unternehmen Platz finden und aufsteigen wollen. Denn den guten Ruf der dualen Absolventen, den habe er schon gespürt. „Es eilt einem voraus, dass man das geschafft hat." Er selbst blieb nicht bei seiner Firma, sondern machte noch seinen Master, an einer australischen Universität. „Ich wollte noch mal an eine normale Uni, mit Studentenleben und Büchern, in die man sich vertieft", sagt er. Ein anderes Unternehmen, das ihn bereits während seiner Ausbildung abwerben wollte, nahm ihn auch noch nach zwei Jahren.

Der weiterführende Abschluss steht nicht jedem offen. Die Masterfrage gehört zu den Nachteilen, die neben der hohen Arbeitsbelastung, der (zu?) frühen Bindung an ein bestimmtes Unternehmen und der mangelnden Wissenschaftlichkeit des Studiums zu den meistgenannten Nachteilen der dualen Abschlüsse gehört. Bei vielen Unternehmen muss sich der Auszubildende verpflichten, nach dem Bachelor zwei, drei oder sogar fünf Jahre im Betrieb zu bleiben. Schließlich investieren die Firmen sehr viel Geld in ihre zukünftigen Mitarbeiter. 948 Millionen Euro im Jahr geben Unternehmen derzeit für die dualen Studenten aus – und erwarten dafür, dass sich der maßgeschneiderte Nachwuchs anschließend entsprechend einbringt. Torsten Licht musste keine Verpflichtung unterschreiben, aber viele seiner Kollegen. Brach einer das Studium frühzeitig ab, musste er die bereits gezahlten Studiengebühren zurückzahlen.

Wer also schon weiß, dass er nach dem Bachelor weiter studieren will, sollte das Dualstudium überdenken. Zwar gibt es die Möglichkeit, den Master als Fernstudium oder Abendstudium zu absolvieren. Doch das bedeutet natürlich weitere Jahre ohne Wochenenden, freie Abende und Ferien.

Viele duale Studenten werden zu Führungskräften ausgebildet, mit entsprechendem Arbeitspensum. Wer das jedoch zum Ziel hat und dabei den schnellen Weg nehmen will, ist mit dem dualen Studium gut bedient. Für Philipp Mertens stand von Anfang an fest, dass ein herkömmliches Hochschulstudium ihm zu wenig

Praxis bietet. Er wählte den Studiengang BWL mit Schwerpunkt Groß- und Außenhandel an der Berufsakademie in Eisenach und arbeitete im 12-Wochen-Takt bei einer Baumarktkette. „Mir war es wichtig, nicht die ganze Zeit die Schulbank zu drücken", sagt er, „der regelmäßige Wechsel zwischen Arbeiten und Lernen war wunderbar."

Auch Mertens betont den Stress dieser drei Jahre, zudem sei es finanziell trotz guten Gehalts von 800 Euro brutto im ersten, 1 000 Euro im zweiten und 1 200 Euro im dritten Jahr manchmal eng gewesen. Schließlich fordert das duale Studium wie in seinem Fall häufig eine Unterkunft an zwei Orten. Doch Disziplin und Entbehrungen haben sich ausgezahlt. Wie vom Studenten gewünscht und vom Unternehmen angestrebt, hat Mertens heute eine Führungsposition.

3 Neither here nor there

Getting started

A1 Think about the different aspects of identity reflected in the pictures.
Find a suitable heading for each of them.

A2 Group work: Placemat:
a) Write down three aspects of identity which are most important for you and explain your choice. You can use ideas from the pictures or your own.

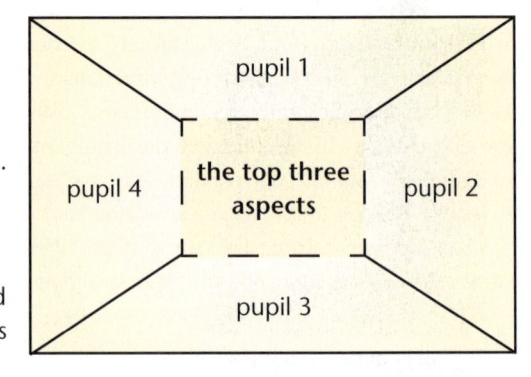

b) Rotate the placemat and write down your comments on the ideas of the others.

c) Finally discuss your ideas in the group and agree on the group's top three aspects.

Neither here nor there: Living in a multicultural society

3

A3 a) Choose one quotation and explain its meaning in your own words.

b) Present your explanations to the class.

1. "The identity of one changes with how one perceives reality."
   *(Vithu Jeyaloganathan, Canadian composer, *1991)*

2. "I think history is inextricably linked to identity. If you don't know your history, if you don't know your family, who are you?" *(Mary Pipher, US clinical anthropologist, *1947)*

3. "Work is an essential part of being alive. Your work is your identity. It tells you who you are."
   *(Kay Stepkin, US baker, *1942)*

4. "Your identity and your success go hand in hand. Many people sacrifice their identities by not doing what they really want to do. And that's why they're not successful."
   *(Lila Swell, professor of education, Columbia University, *1964)*

5. "An identity would seem to be arrived at by the way in which the person faces and uses his experience." *(James Baldwin, US writer, 1924–1987)*

6. "A racial community provides not only a sense of identity, that luxury of looking into another's face and seeing yourself reflected back, but a sense of security and support." *(Wentworth Miller, US actor, *1972)*

7. "A wife should no more take her husband's name than he should hers. My name is my identity and must not be lost." *(Lucy Stone, US abolitionist and suffragist, 1818–1893)*

A4 Pair work: Discuss the statements you most/least agree with.

Practice section

Pre-reading

B1 Growing up in a multicultural environment is not always easy, as you may encounter people with different cultural backgrounds, different habits and customs, or different value systems.

The first person narrator of the novel "(Un)arranged marriage" by Bali Rai, Manjit, is a teenage boy from a traditional Punjabi family. They live in Leicester in the East Midlands.

Think-pair-share: Speculate on the problems he may be confronted with in his family.

Comprehension: Analyzing characters

B2 a) Read the extract from Rai's novel. Describe your first impression of Manjit and outline his situation.

b) Explain which of the quotations – if any – from A3 on page 49 best describes Manjit's attitude.

Extract from "(Un)arranged marriage" by Bali Rai

[…] And my dad, well, he ran the family with fear. He was always either at work or sitting around, pissed[1] on Teacher's whisky, shouting at everyone. He got angry all the time, maybe at
5 something he'd seen on the TV or some problem at work, or sometimes for no reason at all. I'd never seen him hit my mum or anything like that. With her and my sister-in-law he just shouted a lot which scared them enough
10 anyway. I had seen him hit my brothers though, whenever they were out of order[2], which was not that often because they were basically turning into newer versions of him and that was what he wanted all his sons to be.
15 With me though it was like open season[3]. He'd hit me for asking him too many questions or for daring to say something back to him. One time, he'd clipped me round the head for having a go at Harry, and I had answered back calling
20 him a "bastard". I got beaten that day with his old hockey stick that he kept under the stairs and I had to tell everyone at school that I hurt myself playing football. He hit me all the time, sometimes I reckon just because I was in
25 his range. It was either his fists or his feet or anything hard that came to hand. Not that I was that bothered by it. I mean, he'd been doing it since I was a kid and I just saw it as one of the daily hazards of growing up – trying to avoid
30 getting hit. I did wonder though why he singled me out. Sometimes I thought it was because I was the youngest and other times I really thought that he hated me for some reason, only I was never told what it was. Maybe he could see
35 that I was more influenced by the whole Western culture thing than my brothers had been. He definitely didn't like the fact that my best friend wasn't Asian. Either way, getting hit all the time made me feel an outsider and the feeling just got
40 stronger as I grew older.

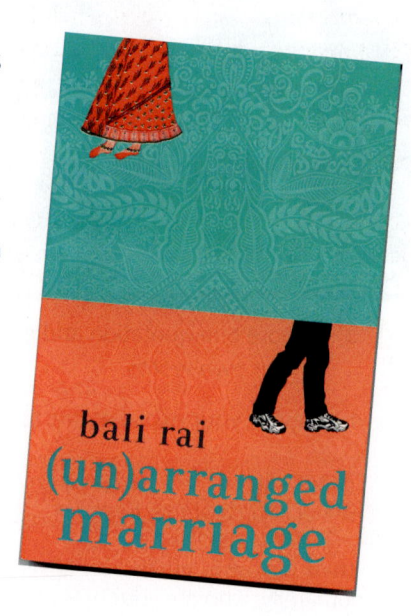

---

[1] **to be pissed** (sl) = to be drunk
[2] **out of order** = behaviour that is out of order is annoying because it is not suitable for a particular situation
[3] **open season** = the period during which it is legal to hunt; (infml) a time of unrestrained harassment, criticism, or attack

Neither here nor there: Living in a multicultural society

We lived on Evington Drive, in an area that was popular with Punjabi families. There were only three bedrooms which meant that I had to move out of my box room and in with Harry when Ranjit got married and his wife moved in with us. Ranjit and Jas got my old room, even though it only just had room for their bed, but that was their problem. They were the ones who had nicked[4] my room from me.

Sharing a room with Harry was like my worst nightmare. He was fat and hairy, and had a horrible habit of leaving his dirty football kit, muddy boots included, all over the place. He only bathed every three days and in the summer the room stank of stale sweat when he'd been lifting weights. At night I used to pretend that he wasn't there by pulling the duvet over myself like a tent and reading by torchlight. Even then he'd throw things at me or call me a poof[5].

"What you wanna read for, man? Bloody Dickens – what are you, a gorah (white) or something? Read about bloody man's stuff, innit[6]."

I hated having no privacy, no time to myself that wasn't intruded on by a brother who still found fart jokes incredibly funny. He was so bloody thick[7], it was like talking to a gorilla sometimes. I hated him. And he'd turn up like a bad smell every time I wanted some peace, no matter where I was – the garden, the garage, wherever. Recently Ranjit and his wife had started doing the same, always around and giggling at each other like kids.

My mum was always in the kitchen, cooking, or watching the Asian channels on Sky in the living room. And Dad? Well, he was a law unto himself, walking around the house like a drunken zombie, belching all the time. To escape, I'd tried locking myself in the bathroom once but only succeeded in getting a smack in the mouth from him for my trouble. I couldn't even do my homework in peace because no-one in my family saw it as being important. They thought that school was a waste of time, like quite a lot of working-class Punjabi families. All they were interested in was trying to earn money and you couldn't do that at school or college. Ranjit and Harry had both got jobs in factories as soon as they left school. It was a wonder that I ever got the high grades that I did – not that anyone in my family cared. [...]

[4] **to nick** (infml) = to steal
[5] **poof** (offensive sl) = a homosexual male
[6] **innit** (infml) = used as a general question tag after any statement, especially by young British Asians
[7] **thick** (infml) = here: stupid

Neither here nor there: Living in a multicultural society

Analysis

B3 a) Imagine you want to describe your best friend. Note down the points you would talk about.

b) Compare your results with a partner and find categories for describing someone.

B4 Manjit is a fictional construct in a novel, not a real person. To understand him better you must have a closer look at the extract and find certain features of his character. In the following grid you will find either a definition of a certain aspect or a quotation. Complete the grid.

aspect and definition/explanation	example
1.	2. "[W]hat are you, a gorah (white) …]?" (ll. 61-62).
3. Personality/Character traits Characters in a novel, as well as real-life people, have unique attributes describing their personality, e.g. (in)tolerance, openness, (dis)honesty etc.	4.
5.	6. "At night I used to pretend that he wasn't there by pulling the duvet over myself […] and reading by torchlight" (ll. 56-58).
7. Mood This describes the emotional state a person or character in a novel is in, e.g. (un)happiness.	8.
9. Language/Idiolect This refers to the way a character in a novel talks, uses grammar, vocabulary and pronounces words, which provides information about social background, education and attitudes etc.	10.
11.	12. "They [Manjit's family] thought that school was a waste of time, like quite a lot working-class Punjabi families" (ll. 83-85).
13. Relations to others This describes the social relations the character has with others – how does he/she interact with others, how do others interact with him/her and see him/her?	14.
15. Function for the story It is important to look at the function a character has for the story he/she is part of – is he/she the protagonist, a main or a minor character, is he/she the narrator etc.?	16.

Neither here nor there: Living in a multicultural society

Info: Types of character and characterization

In a novel you will find different types of character:

round character	flat character
• dynamic character	• static character
• complex	• simple
• develops throughout the novel	• does not change
• unpredictable	• predictable

A character in a fictional text may be presented in different ways:

Telling technique: direct characterization	Showing technique: indirect (dramatic) characterization
The author tells the reader directly and explicitly about the character's looks, traits, attitudes. This can be done by the narrator, the character himself/herself or other characters. Example: "He [Harry] only bathed every three days and in the summer the room stank" (ll.53-55). However, this information may not always be reliable. Since the statements represent the views of different characters, they need not be entirely true, they may be influenced positively by love, or negatively by feelings like jealousy or envy.	You learn a lot about a character by studying what he/she says and does, how he/she behaves in certain situations and interacts with others. The reader is invited to infer traits from the character's action, clothing and body language; he/she must find out for himself/herself. Example: "'What you wanna read for, man? Bloody Dickens – what are you, a gorah [...] or something? Read about bloody man's stuff, innit'" (ll. 60-63). → Harry does not speak proper English, even though he has lived in Britain for a long time. He does not want to integrate into British society. → Harry does not value British culture; here represented by the famous British author Charles Dickens. → Harry has very traditional views on how a man should behave.

B5 a) Look at the highlighted passages in the extract from "(Un)arranged marriage" below. In the parts highlighted in green Manjit characterizes himself directly. Note down what you find out about him here.

b) The blue passages are examples of indirect characterization. Note down what is revealed about Manjit here.

"I was more influenced by the whole Western culture thing than my brothers had been. [...] [G]etting hit all the time made me feel an outsider and the feeling just got stronger as I grew older" (ll. 35-40).

"I couldn't even do my homework in peace because no-one in my family saw it as being important. All they were interested in was trying to earn money and you couldn't do that at school or college. Ranjit and Harry had both got jobs in factories as soon as they left school" (ll. 85-89).

Neither here nor there: Living in a multicultural society

B6 Analyze the remaining text to find out more about Manjit. Collect information from the text in a grid. For your grid use the categories from B4 on page 52.

category	direct / explicit	indirect / implicit	interpretation
...			
relation to others		"My mum was always in the kitchen, cooking, or watching the Asian channels on Sky in the living room" (ll. 74-76)	Apparently, Manjit does not have much in common with his mother; he seems to see her activities/pastimes as dull or monotonous.
...			

Skills: How to quote p. 135

B7 Use your results from B4 to B6 to write a detailed characterization of Manjit. Remember to provide evidence for your findings by referring to and quoting from the text. Follow these steps to plan and write your characterization:

1. **Introduction:** State who you are writing about and what the focus of your analysis will be.

2. **Main part:** Use the categories of characterization to organize the main part by topic. This is preferable to a chronological order as working through the text chronologically often produces unnecessary repetitions.

3. **Conclusion:** At the end, present the main points of your findings in a precise and convincing manner.

Skills: How to structure a text pp. 138-141

Language support: characterization		
introduction	main part	conclusion
• Manjit, the protagonist of the novel, describes his life and circumstances in his family and reveals that his relationship to his family is an unhappy one. • Manjit, the first-person narrator of the story, seems to be troubled with his life as the child of very traditional Punjabi immigrants in England's Western culture.	• The character is presented/described as .../in a ... way. • His body language reveals/suggests ... • When he claims that/comments on/protests that ..., it becomes obvious that ... • The fact that he ... (action) reveals/highlights/underlines that ...	• As a result of the analysis, Manjit can be described as ... • The detailed characterization proves that ... but at the same time ... • The essential outcome of my analysis is that Manjit is actually ...

Analysis

Identifying narrative perspective

B8 There are different ways to tell a story. The author has a choice of different narrative perspectives: Depending on the point of view from which the story is told the story may have an entirely different effect on the reader.

a) Read the info-box to find out about different narrative perspectives.
b) Identify the narrative perspective in Bali Rai's "(Un)arranged marriage".
c) Compare the passage from the novel to the altered versions on page 56 and point out differences and their effect on the reader.

Info: Narrative Perspective

1. First person narration
A first person narrator uses *I* and *me* and is usually the novel's central character but may also be a minor character who merely observes the action. The reader can easily identify with the first person narrator, but since the narrator provides a very personal, subjective view of events including his/her own feelings the information may not always be reliable.

2. Third person narration
A third person narrator is not part of the story, so the characters in the story are referred to as *he, she, they*. The third person narrator can be either omniscient or limited:

a) omniscient narrator
The omniscient narrator knows everything about his characters. He can look inside their minds and knows their thoughts and feelings. He may comment on events and/or the behaviour of his characters or he may choose to merely report without an explicit comment. He also knows how the plot will develop and can switch between places and times. Thus he can refer to past events in a flashback or foreshadow future developments in the plot.

The omniscient narrator may be
- **intrusive**: He comments directly on events and the behaviour of his characters, often providing a moral judgement or highlighting the general importance of the story.
- **unintrusive**: Even though the narrator has insight into the thoughts and feelings of his characters, he merely reports them without an explicit comment.

b) limited narrator
The limited narrator's insight into thoughts and feelings is restricted to one of the characters. He sees and judges the development of the story through the eyes of that particular character only.

3. Multiple narrators
The story is told by different characters in the novel so that the events are seen from different perspectives. Thus the reader is presented with different views of an event and the reasons behind it, as each narrator contributes new aspects. This perspective is frequently used in modern novels.

3 Neither here nor there: Living in a multicultural society

Text A
[...] And my dad, well, he ran the family with fear. He was always either at work or sitting around, pissed on Teacher's whisky, shouting at everyone. He got angry all the time, maybe at something he'd seen on the TV or some problem at work, or sometimes for no reason at all. I'd never seen him hit my mum or anything like that. With her and my sister-in-law he just shouted a lot which
5 scared them enough anyway. I had seen him hit my brothers though, whenever they were out of order, which was not that often because they were basically turning into newer versions of him and that was what he wanted all his sons to be.

Text B
His dad was always drunk. Manjit used to sense it as soon as he entered a room even before the abuse started. He hated his father drinking, he hated the shouting that intimidated the whole family – not that his father would ever hit his mother or his sister-in-law, but shouting abuse at them felt as much a violation as did the actual beating Manjit was the prime victim of. Manjit was
5 ashamed of his father and of his own helplessness as he felt a silent anger rise in him. His father didn't even need a reason to beat him. It seemed that Manjit himself was the reason – unlike his brothers who were only hit when they were out of order, Manjit had not turned into a newer version of his father and that was what his father wanted all his sons to be.

Text C
When Manjit's father was drunk sooner or later the shouting would start. His mother would shrink away from the verbal abuse but although she knew that eventually he would take it out on Manjit and start beating him she didn't seem to mind. She was relieved that neither she nor her daughter in law were the victims and wasn't her husband right? He was the head of the household
5 and this was the way it was meant to be. Manjit would simply have to learn to accept it. What Manjit's father resented in him was, that – unlike his brothers - Manjit was not turning into a newer version of him. Like many Punjabi fathers he expected his sons to be like him, but it was obvious that all the beating did not change Manjit into the person his father wanted. On the contrary, Manjit was disgusted by his father and his behaviour, he felt shame and anger rise in him.
10 One day he would either turn against his father or simply walk out.

Creative writing

Checklist:
Creative writing
pp. 128-129

Any creative writing task you will be given in your exam will require that the fictional text you produce is based on what you have previously found out about the original text.

B9 Ranjit, Manjit's older brother, can see that Manjit will not turn into "a newer version" of their father like himself. Talking to a Punjabi friend he complains about Manjit and comments on his father's reaction. Write their dialogue.

> **Checklist**
> *Creative writing*
>
> **What have you found out from the original text?**
> **Content:** Stick to the plot as it has developed up to this point.
> ✓ What has happened so far?
> ✓ What do you know about the character/s?
> ✓ How do they feel about the current problem?
> ✓ What mood are the characters in?
>   → What might the characters' plans/intentions be? How might they react?

Neither here nor there: Living in a multicultural society

Language: Adopt an appropriate register.
- ✓ How does the character speak?
    - → Depending on the point of view of your character, use an appropriate idiolect (register, sentence structure, choice of words).
- ✓ What is typical of the author's style?
    - Is the choice of words simple, sophisticated, scientific?
    - Are the sentences simple or complex?
    - Is the focus on narrative passages or on dialogue?
    - Does the author use imagery in his/her descriptions?
    - Try to imitate these aspects in your text production.

Language support: dialogue

When you write a *dialogue,* remember to use typical features of spoken language like

- elliptical sentences, especially in questions/exclamations: "What? He wouldn't. Never."
- question tags: "He's never understood me, has he?"
- hesitation devices: "Well, ...", "Basically ...", "Actually ...", "You know ..."
- colloquial language (if appropriate for the speakers involved and the given situation): "I'm gonna ...", "He ain't ..."
- contact clauses: "She is the girl I have been looking for."

These features apply to dialogues in a prose text, plays or film scripts. They can also be used in a diary entry, an interior monologue or even in an informal letter since these forms imitate spoken language.

You have gained some insight into Manjit's character. Use your knowledge of Manjit to turn the last three paragraphs of the extract into a story told from the point of view of a third person limited narrator who focuses his interest on Manjit.

Language support

Use phrases that show that the narrator can read Manjit's thoughts and inner feelings:
- he often thought/ wondered/ imagined/ doubted/ felt/ knew
- he simply couldn't understand why ... / wasn't sure how long ...
- he had turned into ... / they had made him ... / he would soon ...

Use words that comment on his situation or sum it up:
- hopeless / misunderstood / isolated / lonely / superior / self-confident /
- as ..., the situation became more and more difficult/ unbearable / too frustrating

Compare him to his family:
- While / even though / instead / and yet / not that ...

Find alternative formulations and combine them with a comment:
- not that anyone cared
    - → his family seemed entirely indifferent to his efforts and it was a shame that they cared so little about the achievements of the youngest member of the family

3

Neither here nor there: Living in a multicultural society

Getting to the point

Pre-reading

C1 The terrorist attack of 9/11 and 7/7 have greatly changed the quality of our lives especially in multi-cultural societies.

Think-pair-share: Speculate on how multi-cultural societies might be affected.

> **Info:**
> 9/11 stands for the terrorist attacks on the World Trade Center in New York and on the Pentagon on September 11, 2001. Al Qaida terrorists hijacked planes and flew them into the twin towers of the World Trade Center, which caught fire and collapsed and resulted in the death of almost 3000 people. These attacks had a serious impact on the American people and triggered a world wide war on terrorism.
>
> 7/7: The London bombings of July 7, 2005 are often referred to as 7/7. In coordinated suicide attacks on three underground trains and a London bus 52 people were killed and more than 700 wounded.

Comprehension

C2 Anna Perera's novel "Guantanamo Boy", 2009 (shortlisted for the Costa Children's Book Award) deals with fifteen-year-old Khalid, who lives in Manchester with his family. His parents are from Pakistan but, just like his father, Khalid has English friends, likes playing football in the park and feels more English than Pakistani.

Read the extract from the novel and outline the situation that changes Khalid's life, his understanding of himself and his social identity.

Extract from "Guantanamo Boy" by Anna Perera

'By the way,' Holgy says, laughing, 'Mikael's parents are bunking off somewhere on Saturday so he's having a party.'
Khalid's about to get the details, as he's
5 never been to Mikael's before, when a commotion starts up outside the fish-and-chip shop a few doors down. A slim woman in a grey tracksuit and trainers, about thirty years old, is arguing with the steroid heads[1]
10 from school.
A slightly tubby[2] kid swigs[3] from a bottle of beer. Behaving like an idiot, he starts jumping up and down as if bouncing on a trampoline, while the others surround the
15 woman, grabbing her chips and flinging them in the air. 'There goes another one – wooeee!'
Taunting[4] her with a blizzard of daft[5] hand movements, they pump her space with their
20 shoulders so one of them can dip his hand in her tracksuit pocket to steal her mobile.
They're at it again, thinks Khalid. 'Hey!' he screams at the top of his voice. Being the kind of kid who likes a beer now and then, has
25 stolen a couple of things from the stalls down the market for a bet, he often finds himself pretending to be wilder, more confident and stronger than he really is to prove he can hold his own with some of the
30 older kids. But today resentment at the steroid heads' stupid behaviour rises in him like never before.
Holgy and Tony laugh their heads off as Khalid angrily runs over to push the kids
35 aside. 'Give it here!' He knocks the mobile out of the little fair-haired one's hand, then grabs the bag of chips from the tubby one, who now has them.

---

[1] **steroid head** = bodybuilder; so. who takes steroids
[2] **tubby** = slightly fat
[3] **to swig** = to drink carelessly and in large amounts
[4] **to taunt** = to say or do sth. in order to make so. angry or upset
[5] **daft** = silly

'Sorry,' Khalid tells the woman as he hands
40 back the phone. 'They're a bunch of losers.'
   She thanks him briefly with a nod and refuses the remaining chips with a sour expression. Gives him the feeling she doesn't want his help, then strides off proudly,
45 swishing her ponytail as if she was never in any danger in the first place.
   'Whaddya do that for?' One of the kids frowns. 'We were only having a bit of fun.'
   'Push off, you jerk!' Khalid says. 'Do that
50 again and I'll thump[6] you.'
   When he turns back to Holgy and Tony, they are still killing themselves laughing.
   'What are you like? Fess up[7], Kal. Didn't you see – ha-ha-ha – how pale she went –
55 ha-ha – when you screamed at them?' Holgy says.
   'I mean, you're pretty tall, Kal. She was more scared of you than – ha-ha – of that lot.'

'If you had a beard, you'd be a dead
60 ringer[8] for Bin Laden, mate,' Tony adds, and both of them crack up[9] again.
   'Yeah?' Suddenly it dawns on Khalid that the woman maybe thought he was a terrorist or something. 'These are dangerous times for
65 Muslims,' his dad said the other day. And he was right. That much he does know. [...]
   Hands tucked deep in his pockets, Khalid stands under the green canvas of the shop, staring at the display of grapefruits,
70 cabbages, tomatoes, peppers, ginger and garlic, suddenly unable to remember why he's here. Unable to remember anything but the look of contempt[10] on the slim woman's face and Tony's words, which he knows were
75 supposed to be a joke, but even so … It's the first time world events and George Bush's so-called 'War on Terror' really come home to[11] him.

[6] **to thump** = to hit
[7] **to fess up** = to admit that you have done sth. wrong
[8] **dead ringer for so.** = so. who looks exactly like so. else
[9] **to crack up** = to start laughing
[10] **contempt** = feeling that so. is unimportant or worthless
[11] **to come home to** = to make so. realize the full significance of sth.

Analysis

C3 Compare the narrative perspective of the text to the one in Bali Rai's "(Un-)arranged marriage".

C4 Analyze how direct and indirect characterization are used to reveal the difference between Khalid's true character and the prejudice he is confronted with.

Skills
Checklist:
Text analysis
p. 125

Comment

C5 Consider the woman's reaction and Holgy's comment and discuss the possible consequences for Khalid's future behaviour.

Skills
Checklist:
Comment
pp. 126-127

Creative writing

C6 Choose either Khalid or the woman and tell the story from the point of view of a first person narrator. Make sure you include all the necessary details and present them in an appropriate register.

Skills
Checklist:
Creative writing
pp. 128-129

4 Think before you post

Getting started

A1 a) Think about how much time you spend on the Internet and what you use it for. Note down your results.

b) Compare your notes in small groups.

A2 Study the cartoon and say what makes it funny.

> **Tip**
> It is usually the combination of visual elements and text in a cartoon that creates a humorous effect.

"I love our nights in together, just you, me, and our 756 friends."

A3 Think-pair-share: First note down your ideas and then talk about
- why people use chat rooms
- what makes chat rooms attractive
- what problems users might be confronted with.

A4 a) Read the two extracts and say what experiences Amy (Extract 1) and Jeni (Extract 2) have while chatting online.

b) Add any new information to your notes in A3.

Extract 1 from "Amy" by Mary Hooper
[Amy (Buzybee) meets Zed in a chat room on the Internet.]

"It all started after I fell out with Louise and Bethany, really. It was falling out with them that made me find friends somewhere else, and the Internet seemed a good place to look. I mean everyone wants friends, don't they?" [...]

Think before you post: Dangers of the Internet

[Soon they start chatting one to one outside the chat room and even exchange photographs.]

B: Love the photo. I've got it by my bed.
Z: Yours is GR8. You're a babe[1]!
B: Was yours taken in the office!
Z: Yeah. It was for the salesman of the week board. [...]

B: Have U ever been at the top?
Z: Loads of times. I'm brilliant at selling!
B: I'd be useless.
Z: Hey – U look GR8 in your photo, but it's only head shoulders. What about the rest of U!
B: What about it?
Z: Your figure?
B: I go in and out a bit!
Z: I need 2 know more than that if I'm going 2 get the full picture. I like 2 fantasise! So how about giving me your bust size?
B: 34.
Z: Cup size?
B: B.
Z: OK! Hang on a sec – I'm going to close my eyes and think about U. [...]
Z: How about us 2 getting together some time?
B: You mean meet up 4 real?
Z: Right. U could come down here 4 the day. Stay the night with me.

Extract 2 from "Fever of the Bone" by Val McDermid

[The police are investigating the murder of Jennifer Maidment.]

"According to Claire Darsie, her and Jennifer used Rigmarole[1] all the time. And Gary here's been able to pull up[2] a whole stack[3] of their chat room and IM[4] sessions."
"Anything useful?" [...]
"There's a lot of rubbish," Gary said. "The usual teenage chatter about X Factor and Big Brother. Pop stars and soap actors. Gossip[5] about their mates[6] from school. Mostly they're talking to other kids in their class, but there are some outsiders from other areas of Rigmarole." [...]
"And then it gets really interesting," Gary said [...].
"This was five days ago."

Jeni: Wot do u mean, zz?
ZZ: Evry1 has secrets, things theyr ashamed of. Things u'd die if ur crew new about.
Jeni: I don't. My best friend nos everything about me.
ZZ: That's wot we all say and we all lying.

[...] "... then ZZ pulls Jennifer into a private IM session. Here we go[7]."

ZZ: I wanted 2 talk 2 u in priv8.
Jeni: Y?
ZZ: cuz I no u hav a BIG secret.
Jeni: U no more than me then.
ZZ: sumtimes we don't know wot our own secrets r. Bt I no a secret tt u wd not want anybody else to no.
Jeni: I don't know wot u r on about[8].
ZZ: b online 2moro same time & we'll talk abt it sum more.

---

[1] **You're a babe** = you look fantastic

[1] **Rigmarole** = fictional chat room/social network
[2] **to pull up sth.** = here: to find sth.
[3] **a stack of** = a lot of
[4] **IM session** = instant messaging
[5] **gossip** = conversation about unimportant subjects
[6] **mate** (infml) = friend
[7] **here we go** = here it is
[8] **wot u r on about** = what you are talking about

4   Think before you post: Dangers of the Internet

Practice section

Comprehension: Cartoons

B1 Look at the cartoon "The Dangers of the Internet" below. Write down in one sentence why Colin uses the Internet and what the consequences are.

Analysis: Cartoons

Skills: How to work with cartoons p. 134

B2 Analyze the cartoon below.
When analyzing a cartoon you have to follow these steps:
- Identify the main visual and textual elements: caricature, caption, focal point, etc. (see B2a) below).
- Explain the effect these elements create (see B2a) below).
- State the cartoonist's message and say what makes the cartoon funny.

a) In order to identify the main visual and textual elements and to describe their effect complete the grid below. Match the elements (beige) with their descriptions (green) and the effect created (blue).

b) Now use your sentence from B1 and the information from B2a) to write an analysis of the cartoon.

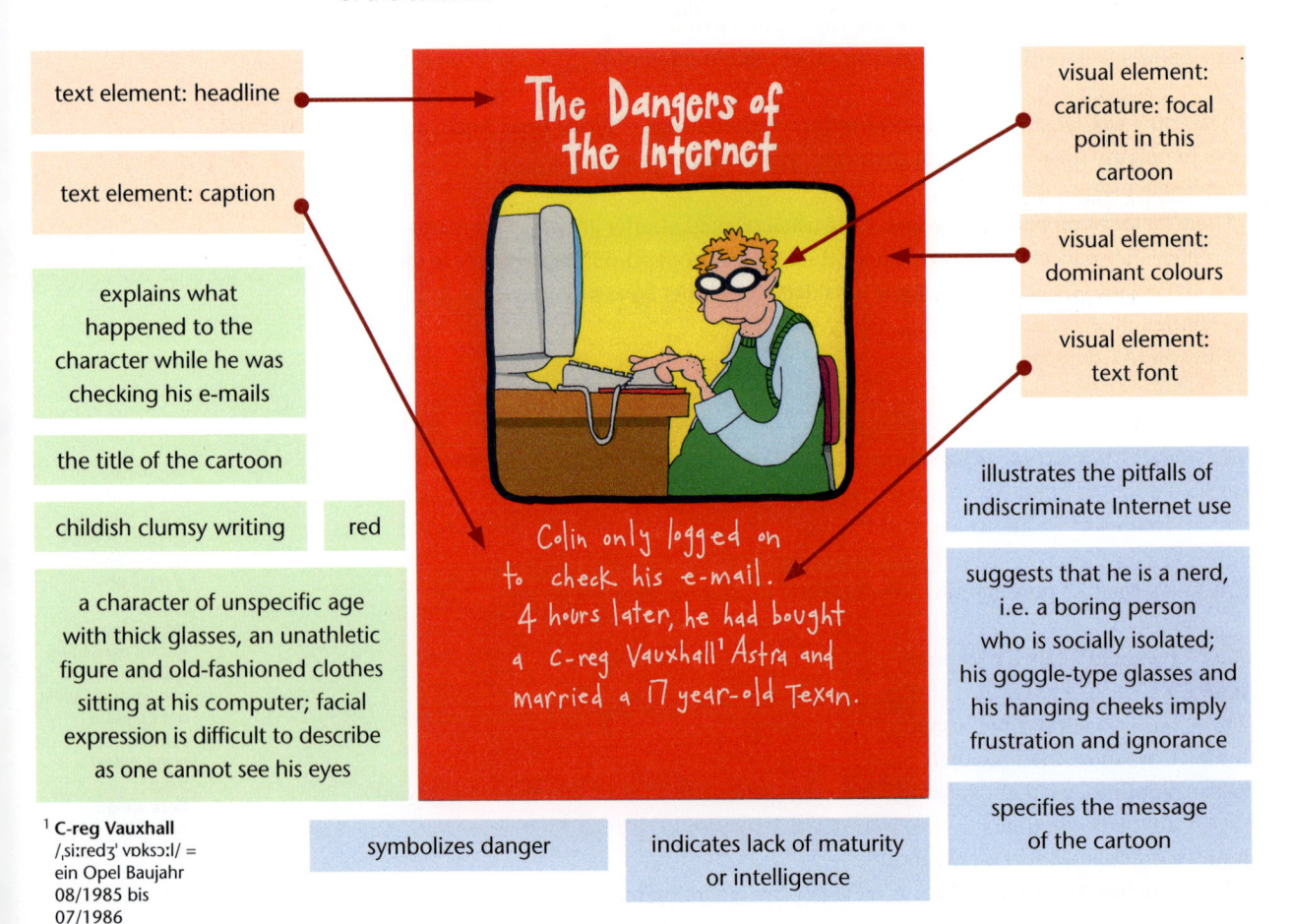

---

text element: headline

text element: caption

visual element: caricature: focal point in this cartoon

visual element: dominant colours

visual element: text font

explains what happened to the character while he was checking his e-mails

the title of the cartoon

childish clumsy writing   red

a character of unspecific age with thick glasses, an unathletic figure and old-fashioned clothes sitting at his computer; facial expression is difficult to describe as one cannot see his eyes

illustrates the pitfalls of indiscriminate Internet use

suggests that he is a nerd, i.e. a boring person who is socially isolated; his goggle-type glasses and his hanging cheeks imply frustration and ignorance

specifies the message of the cartoon

symbolizes danger   indicates lack of maturity or intelligence

Cartoon text: "The Dangers of the Internet. Colin only logged on to check his e-mail. 4 hours later, he had bought a C-reg Vauxhall¹ Astra and married a 17 year-old Texan."

¹ C-reg Vauxhall /ˌsiːredʒ ˈvɒksɔːl/ = ein Opel Baujahr 08/1985 bis 07/1986

Think before you post: Dangers of the Internet

terms: visual elements	description	effect
dominant colours	red	symbolizes danger
...		
terms: text elements		
...		

B3 a) Have a look at the cartoons on page 64 and write down in one sentence what each one is about (introductory sentence).

b) Choose one of the cartoons and find two or three other students who picked the same one. Follow the steps in the checklist to prepare your analysis.

c) Use the information you collected in your group to write a complete analysis on your own.

Checklist:
Text analysis
p. 125

> **Language support**
> The cartoon depicts/illustrates/shows …
> The caption suggests/underlines/implies …
> The figures in the cartoon represent/symbolize …
> The cartoonist visualizes/makes fun of/ridicules …
> The message of the cartoon is accentuated/illustrated by …

> **Checklist**
> ✓ State the topic dealt with in the cartoon in one sentence (introduction).
> ✓ Identify the most important visual and textual elements and describe them.
> ✓ Explain their effects.
> ✓ Consider what makes the cartoon humorous.
> ✓ State the cartoonist's message.
> ✓ Use appropriate vocabulary. Look at the language support box.

4 Think before you post: Dangers of the Internet

1 "But... your Facebook profile says you're a vegetarian!"

2 "We usually shop in the comfort of our own home but the bloody computer crashed"

3 "If you didn't have Facebook when you were a kid, how did you know who your friends were?"

4 "YOUR MOTHER AND I FOUND OUT YOU'VE BEEN BLOGGING. WE DON'T KNOW WHAT THAT MEANS, BUT WE'D LIKE YOU TO STOP."

Comprehension: Non-fictional texts

B4 Read the article "NJ student's suicide illustrates Internet dangers" by Geoff Mulvihill and Samantha Henry and state the authors' attitude towards the Internet in one or two sentences.

In order to do this follow these steps:

- Look at the headline and say what it suggests about the theme of the article.
- Find and note down any parts of the text in which the authors state their attitude or reveal their stance.

NJ student's suicide illustrates Internet dangers

The Washington Post

By GEOFF MULVIHILL and SAMANTHA HENRY

PISCATAWAY, N.J. (AP) – The shocking suicide of a college student whose sex life was broadcast over the Web illustrates yet again the Internet's alarming potential as a means of tormenting others and raises questions whether young people in the age of Twitter and Facebook can even distinguish public from private. Cruel gossip and vengeful acts once confined to the schoolyard or the dorm can now make their way around the world instantly via the Internet, along with photos and live video.

"It's just a matter of when the next suicide's going to hit, when the next attack's going to hit," said Parry Aftab, a New Jersey lawyer who runs the website WiredSafety.

Last week, Rutgers University freshman Tyler Clementi jumped to his death from the George Washington Bridge after his roommate and another classmate allegedly used a webcam to secretly broadcast his dorm room sexual encounters with another man. The two classmates have been charged[1] with invasion of privacy, with the most serious charges carrying[2] up to five years in prison.

The suicide of Clementi, a shy, gifted 18-year-old violinist, shocked and disturbed gay rights activists and others on campus. "Had he been in bed with a woman, this would not have happened," said Rutgers student Lauren Felton, 21, of Warren, N.J. "He wouldn't have been outed via an online broadcast, and his privacy would have been respected and he might still have his life."

The Associated Press found at least 12 cases in the U.S. since 2003 in which children and young adults between 11 and 18 killed themselves after falling victim to some form of "cyber-bullying" – teasing, harassing or intimidating with pictures or words distributed online or via text message. In probably the best-known case, 13-year-old Megan Meier of Daddenne Prairie, Mo., hanged herself in 2006 after she received messages on MySpace – supposedly from a teenage boy – cruelly dumping[3] her. An adult neighbor was later found guilty of taking part in the hoax[4], but the conviction was overturned[5].

Earlier this year, 17-year-old Alexis Pilkington of West Islip, N.Y., who had landed[6] a college soccer scholarship, killed herself after receiving a stream of nasty messages.

Gregory Jantz, founder of A Place of Hope, a Seattle mental health care center, said young people who use the Internet to spread something damaging about others often don't realize how hurtful it can be because many of them have grown up in a world[7] that has blurred the line between public and private.

"Our kids are in a different zone now," Jantz said. Aftab said young people who would never bully someone face to face do it online in part because of the often-false sense of anonymity that the Internet provides[8]. "They'll also jump on because they don't want to be the next target," Aftab said.

In Clementi's case, prosecutors said that his roommate, Dharun Ravi of Plainsboro, N.J., and Molly Wei of Princeton, N.J., both 18-year-old freshmen, transmitted a live image of Clementi having sex on Sept. 19 and that Ravi tried to webcast a second encounter on Sept. 21, the day before Clementi's suicide. Ravi's lawyer and a lawyer believed to be representing Wei did not return calls.

The mourning[9] continued at Rutgers; in Ridgewood, the suburban New Jersey town where Clementi grew up and attended high school; [...] Childhood friend Mary Alcaro, who played in a summer music academy with him, said Clementi had been destined[10] for greatness. "I've never heard anyone make a violin sing the way he did," she said in an e-mail. [...]

Students at West Windsor-Plainsboro Regional High School, from which Ravi and Wei graduated[11], remembered them as nice people who were not in any way homophobic. Ravi had gay friends, said Derek Yan, 16, a junior. Yan said he chatted online with Ravi about what college life was like, and Ravi "said he was lucky to have a good roommate. He said his roommate was cool."

---

[1] **to charge so. with sth.** = *here*: jdn. wegen einer Sache anklagen
[2] **to carry** = *here*: nach sich ziehen
[3] **to dump so.** – to end a romantic/sexual relationship with so.
[4] **hoax** = Täuschung
[5] **to overturn** = *here*: to say officially that sth. is wrong and change it
[6] **to land sth.** = *here*: to gain sth.
[7] **a world that has blurred the line between public and private** = a world where you can no longer tell the difference between public and private
[8] **to provide sth.** = to make sth. available
[9] **mourning** = process of showing great sadness after so.'s death
[10] **destined for sth.** = certain to do sth.
[11] **to graduate** = to finish your studies at a high school

Think before you post: Dangers of the Internet

Analysis: Non-fictional texts

B5 Read the article again. Identify and explain the means the authors use to convey their attitude. When analyzing the authors' intention/point of view, you have to take these aspects into consideration:
- choice of language/words that trigger(s) associations; e.g. the words "shocking", "alarming", "tormenting", "vengeful", "cruel" imply danger;
- quotations to give weight to the arguments, i.e. citing expert opinions or eyewitnesses; e.g. *"The statement of a New Jersey lawyer lends authenticity to the authors' message."*
- facts and figures to back up the arguments by giving evidence;
- information which has an emotional appeal and awakens (human) interest e.g. the terrible loss caused by cyber-bullying and the resulting suicide.

a) Find more examples of these aspects in the text.

b) Assess how far the author's point of view is biased.

Language support: expressing opinions

The author expresses in a ... way
He/She makes a case for/against ...
He/She favours ...
He/She is in favour of ...
He/She is prejudiced against/towards/argues for/against ...
He/She discriminates against ...
He/She indirectly attacks ...
The underlying attitude is ...
He/She seems to be very biased towards ...
He/She shows a very impartial attitude towards ...

Info: Bias

Definition of bias

Bias is a prejudice in favour of or against one thing, person, or group. It is a tendency to hold a certain point of view at the expense of other alternatives.
If an article is biased, it means that information is presented in a one-sided way based on a personal opinion rather than facts.

Detecting bias
- in the headline of an article;
- in the choice of information for an article: what facts/statistics are mentioned/not mentioned, numbers and statistics can be exaggerated or played down in order to influence the reader;
- in the choice of photos and their captions, e.g. photos can flatter a person or ridicule them;
- in the names and descriptions of people indicating bias, e.g. terrorist, ex-convict, call girl;
- in the choice of words. This can be a source of bias. For example, many negative expressions will influence the reader in a particular way.

Comment

B6 Discuss which of the cartoons in B3 on page 64 best illustrates the message of the article. Give reasons.

Think before you post: Dangers of the Internet

4

Getting to the point

Comprehension

C1 Read the article "How dangerous is the Internet for children?" on page 68 by David Pogue and summarize the main points.

Skills
Checklist:
Summary
p. 124

Analysis

C2 Analyze the cartoon below and explain how its message is conveyed.

C3 Analyze the author's point of view in the article and explain the means used to underline it.

Skills
Checklist:
Text analysis
p. 125

Comment

C4 Assess to what extent both the cartoon and the article represent a biased approach towards the Internet.

Skills
Checklist:
Comment
pp. 126-127

67

How dangerous is the Internet for children?

A few years ago, a parenting magazine asked me to write an article about the dangers that children face when they go online. As it turns out[1], I was the wrong author for the article they had in mind[2].

The editor was deeply disappointed by my initial draft. Its chief message was this: "Sure, there are dangers. But they're hugely overhyped by the media. The tales of pedophiles luring children out of their homes are like plane crashes: they happen extremely rarely, but when they do, they make headlines everywhere. [...]"

My editor, however, was looking for something more sensational. [...] So the editor sent me the contact information for several parents of young children with Internet horror stories, and suggested that I interview them. One woman, for example, told me that she became hysterical when her eight-year-old stumbled[3] onto a pornographic photo. She told me that she literally dove[4] for the computer, crashing over a chair, yanking[5] out the power cord and then rushing her daughter outside.

You know what? I think that far more damage was done to that child by her mother's reaction than by the dirty picture.

Now, I realize that not everybody shares my nonchalance[6]. And again, it's not hard to find scattered anecdotes about terrible things that happen online.

But if you live in terror of what the Internet will do to your children, I encourage you to watch this excellent hour long PBS "Frontline" documentary. It's free, and it's online in its entirety. The show surveys the current kids-online situation – thoroughly, open-mindedly and frankly.

Turns out I had it relatively easy writing about the dangers to children under age 12; this documentary focuses on teenagers, 90 percent of whom are online every single day. They are absolutely immersed in chat, Facebook, MySpace and the rest of the Web; it's part of their ordinary social fabric to an extent that previous generations can't even imagine.

The show carefully examines each danger of the Net. And as presented by the show, the sexual-predator thing is way, way[7] overblown[8], just as I had suspected. Several interesting interview transcripts accompany the show online; the one with producer Rachel Dretzin goes like this:

"One of the biggest surprises in making this film was the discovery that the threat of online predators is misunderstood and overblown. The data shows that giving out personal information over the Internet makes absolutely no difference when it comes to a child's vulnerability to predation." (That one blew my mind[9], because every single Internet-safety website and pamphlet hammers repeatedly on this point: never, ever give out your personal information online.)

"Also, the vast majority of kids who do end up having contact with a stranger they meet over the Internet are seeking out that contact," Ms. Dretzin goes on. "Most importantly, all the kids we met, without exception, told us the same thing: They would never dream of meeting someone in person they'd met online."

Several teenagers interviewed in the story make it clear that only an idiot would be lured unwittingly into a relationship with an online sicko[10]: "If someone asks me where I live, I'll delete the 'friend'. I mean, why do you want to know where I live at?" says one girl.

Fearmongers[11] often cite the statistic, from a 2005 study by the Crimes Against Children Research Center, that 1 in 7 children have received sexual propositions while online. But David Finkelhor, author of that report, notes

---

[1] **as it turns out** = wie es sich herausstellt
[2] **to have sth. in mind** = an etwas denken
[3] **to stumble onto sth.** = to find sth. by accident
[4] **dove** = (US) simple past form of dive
[5] **to yank** = to pull sth. with a lot of force
[6] **nonchalance** = feeling relaxed and not worried
[7] **way, way** = (infml) by a very large amount
[8] **overblown** = made to seem more important than it really is
[9] **it blew my mind** = it impressed me very much
[10] **sicko** = so. who likes things that most other people find shocking
[11] **fearmonger** = so. who creates fear

that many of these propositions don't come from Internet predators at all. "Considerable numbers of them are undoubtedly coming from other kids, or just people who are acting weird online," he says.

As my own children approach middle school, my own fears align with the documentary's findings in another way: that cyber-bullying is a far more realistic threat. Kids online experiment with different personas, and can be a lot nastier in the anonymous atmosphere of the Internet than they would ever be in person (just like grown-ups). And their mockery can be far more painful when it's public, permanent and written than if they were just muttered in passing in the hallway.

In any case, watch the show. You'll learn that some fears are overplayed, others are underplayed, and above all, that the Internet plays a huge part in adolescence now. Pining for simpler times is a waste of time; like it or not, this particular genie is out of the bottle.

[12] **to align with sth.** = to match or fit with sth.
[13] **mockery** = Spott
[14] **to pine for sth.** = to be sad because you want sth. you can't have
[15] **this genie is out of the bottle** = it's no longer possible to go back to the old state of affairs on this matter

---

Checklist

Cartoon
- ✓ Write an introductory sentence stating the topic of the cartoon.
- ✓ Describe the most important visual and textual element.
- ✓ Explain their effect.
- ✓ Say what makes the cartoon funny.
- ✓ State the message of the cartoon.

Article
- ✓ Look at the headline to see if it reveals anything about the author's point of view.
- ✓ Read the text once and note down in one or two sentences what the author's point of view is.
- ✓ Read the text carefully and look for evidence to back up your claim e.g. use of language, quotations, facts and figures, emotional appeal.

5 (Anti-) social network

Getting started

A1 a) Collect ways of communicating with your friends. List the uses teens have for electronic media.

b) Compare your findings in class and use them to develop a questionnaire about how you communicate with your friends.

I am ( ) a boy. ( ) a girl.	yes	no
1 I regularly meet my friends in the afternoon/evening and at the weekend.		
...		

I am ( ) a boy. ( ) a girl.	often	sometimes	never
1 I chat with my friends on Facebook.			
...			

c) Conduct a class survey.

d) Point out significant results of the survey and explain them.

A2 a) Look at the statistics on Facebook below and describe them.

b) Explain what they tell you about the development and relevance of Facebook worldwide.

c) Choose one of these Internet research tasks:
  1. Find out what the figures for Facebook and other social networking sites are today, e.g. number and age of users.
     Point out how the use of social networking sites has developed in recent years.
  Or:
  2. Find out about Mark Zuckerberg, how he started Facebook and how his career has developed.

d) Present your results to the class. Discuss whether Zuckerberg deserves the title "Person of the Year" which he was awarded by TIME magazine in 2010.

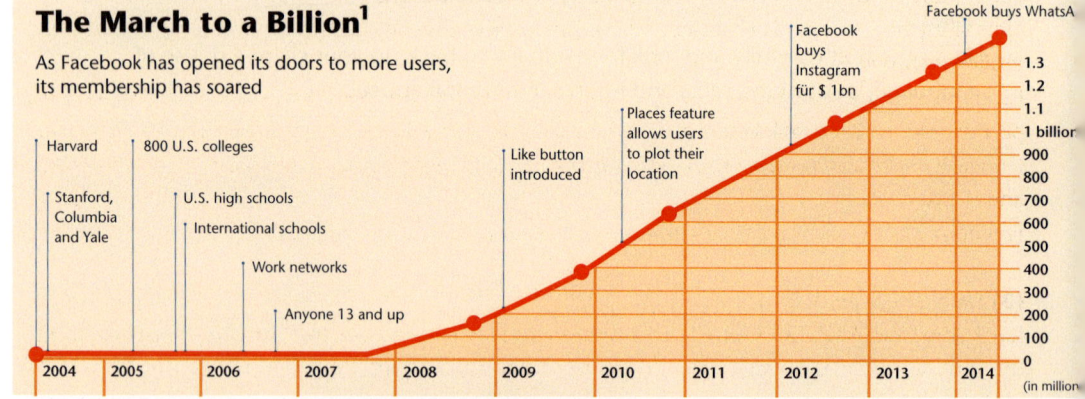

Skills
How to analyze statistics
pp. 150-151

Language support
The horizontal/ vertical axis shows ...
There is a sharp/ rapid/slow/... increase/decline in the number of ...
... is distributed evenly/unevenly among ...
The number of ... reaches a peak/ remains constant/...
Nearly ... % of ...
About a third/ quarter of ...
The majority / minority of ...

[1] 1 US billion = 1,000,000,000

The March to a Billion[1]

As Facebook has opened its doors to more users, its membership has soared

- Harvard
- Stanford, Columbia and Yale
- 800 U.S. colleges
- U.S. high schools
- International schools
- Work networks
- Anyone 13 and up
- Like button introduced
- Places feature allows users to plot their location
- Facebook buys Instagram für $ 1bn
- Facebook buys WhatsA...

2004 2005 2006 2007 2008 2009 2010 2011 2012 2013 2014

1.3 / 1.2 / 1.1 / 1 billion / 900 / 800 / 700 / 600 / 500 / 400 / 300 / 200 / 100 / 0 (in million...)

Facebook friend count

- **15%** Have more than 500 friends
- **39%** Have 1-100 friends
- **23%** Have 251-500 friends
- **23%** Have 101-250 friends

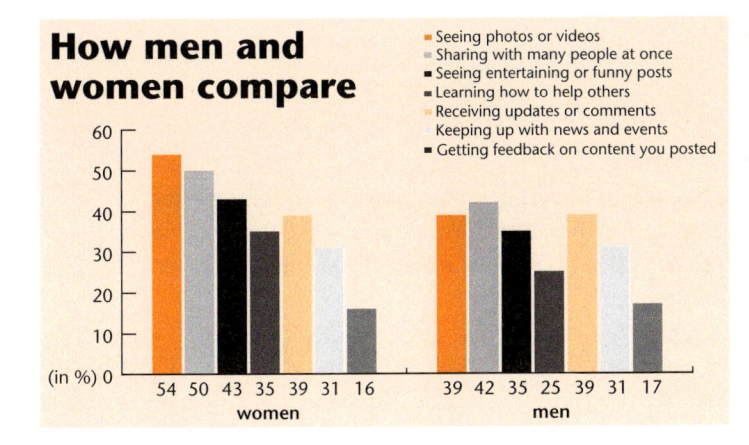

(Anti-) social network: Media and friendship

5

How men and women compare

- Seeing photos or videos
- Sharing with many people at once
- Seeing entertaining or funny posts
- Learning how to help others
- Receiving updates or comments
- Keeping up with news and events
- Getting feedback on content you posted

women: 54 50 43 35 39 31 16
men: 39 42 35 25 39 31 17
(in %)

Person of the Year — TIME — Facebook's Mark Zuckerberg

A3 a) Divide the class into two groups. Read the two texts on the question "Will Facebook conquer the world?" Each group concentrates on one text, either A or B. Make notes on the arguments put forward in favour of/against the extensive use of Facebook.

b) Add more arguments of your own.

c) In class, debate the statement "Making and keeping friends is impossible without Facebook." Note: You should not present your own opinion but stick to the position of your article. Take a vote before the debate on how you see the issue.

d) After the debate, take another vote on the statement in class and discuss whether the debate has changed your view.

How to improve your oral skills pp. 148–149

(A) *Daily Telegraph, Shane Richmond, 04 Jan. 2011*
[…] Facebook is still growing […] and as more join, the network becomes more powerful. Its members aren't just chatting and sharing photos, they are also playing games, reading the news and keeping up with famous people. Facebook Places lets them share their location with friends; Facebook Messages aims to replace our email accounts; and the Facebook experience is now available on more than two million websites. […]
Facebook is more than just a website; it's a mini version of the web. Just as Google dominated the past decade, so Facebook could dominate the coming one. The difference between Facebook and Google is that the latter was only ever a starting point. Facebook is, for many users, the starting point and the destination.
Facebook hasn't just conquered the web, it's becoming a web of its own. […]

(B) *Daily Telegraph, Will Heaven, 04 Jan. 2011*
[…] At the New Year's Eve house party I went to, the response to camera flashes could be heard over the din. "Can we all agree," one girl yelled, "that no one puts these photos on Facebook?" By midnight, the request made perfect sense. Who would want to risk sharing the evening – such as it was – with the entire online world?
For young Facebook users, that is the greatest concern: lack of privacy. The social networking website's Terms of Service are opaque[1]. And even if you manage to understand them, the "privacy" is often an illusion.
While developers quietly delve into your likes and dislikes, all you need to do is post a goofy picture online and before long your trendiest aunt (it was too rude not to accept her "friend request") has emailed it to your parents. Worse still, a friend from work could spot it – and suddenly, seen out of context by other colleagues, a photo lands you in serious trouble. […]

[1] **opaque** = *here:* difficult to understand

5 (Anti-) social network: Media and friendship

Practice section

Pre-viewing

B1 "The Social Network" is a film about Mark Zuckerberg and the development of Facebook. Imagine you are a team of film directors. In groups use the information you have compiled in A2 to plan the opening scene. Outline the scene and present your ideas to the class or to another group.

Comprehension

B2 The film "The Social Network" starts in a Harvard bar with a conversation between Mark and his girlfriend Erica, in which Mark's ambition to make it into the exclusive circles of Harvard becomes obvious; Mark is ditched by his girlfriend who claims that his problem is "not being a nerd but an asshole".

a) Watch extract 1 (5.14 min–8.30 min) which is part of the opening scene of the film, the exposition. Describe how this scene is used to introduce the topic, the setting and the main characters. Pay attention to what expectations are raised.

b) Compare the beginning of the film to your own ideas in B1. Point out the differences and explain what the directors of "The Social Network" might want to communicate by their particular opening.

B3 Watch the sequence again and describe the music that accompanies it. Consider how the combination of music and lighting is employed to create a special atmosphere. With a partner discuss what feelings this evokes in you.

Sound effects/music		
slow piano notes/tempo/ extended pauses unnerving background sounds electronic sound clusters	create(s)	a melancholic/sad mood an aggressive/threatening/eerie atmosphere suspense
dark electronic beats loud low drones monotonous/repetitive rhythm	suggest(s) hint(s) at indicate(s)	an atmosphere of foreboding a feeling of frustration/loneliness/ anger
	signal(s)	a dramatic change in the plot
the depressing mood/feelings of hurt/the negative feelings/ the hidden anger/the desire for revenge	is/are reflected	in the slow pace of the music in the hesitant rhythm the pounding beats
the violin melody	creates	a contrast a happy/cheerful/playful mood
Visual effects/lighting		
the gloomy/shady lighting the darkness the lack of lighting	contributes to underlines/supports corresponds to	the depressive mood the feeling of resentment the dark thoughts of ...
islands of light	are used to create deepen	a contrast the impression of ...

(Anti-) social network: Media and friendship

Analysis

Cinematic devices

B4 Making a film also means using special cinematic devices that carry meaning. This 'film language' is created by the use of camera position or movement and by editing.

a) Read the definitions of different cinematic devices and match them with the film stills on page 74. Be careful: Not all definitions have a photo that goes with them. At the same time some stills may be labelled with two expressions.

b) Explain what the stills reveal about the relationships of the people presented. Consider how relationships or lack of relationships (distance, closeness, loneliness, isolation, superiority) are presented.

Info: Cinematic devices and definitions

cinematic device	definition
camera range / shot size	the distance between the camera and the object filmed
long shot	provides a view of the situation or setting from a distance
full shot	gives a view of the entire figure of a person to show action or to give an impression of a constellation of characters
medium shot	shows a person down to the waist, often used to present two people in conversation
close-up	a full-screen shot of a person's face to show emotions revealed by their facial expression; it can also be used to draw attention to an object that is of particular interest to the plot or has a symbolic function
establishing shot	gives an overall impression of the location at the beginning of a scene
camera angle	the point of view of a camera
high angle shot	the camera looks down on the object so that it seems smaller, less important or inferior
low angle shot	the camera looks up at a person so that people seem more important, powerful or even intimidating as it shows them in a superior position
eye-level shot / straight-on angle	the camera looks straight at the person: this may suggest a neutral view, however, it can also mean that two people who are not on the same level for some reason (e.g. wealth, age, academic standing, social class) are presented as equal to each other
point-of-view	
point-of-view shot	assumes the perspective of one of the characters so that we seem to look through his/her eyes
reverse angle shot	a sequence of point-of-view shots in which the perspective changes from one speaker to the other
camera movement	
panning shot	the camera moves horizontally, i.e. to the left or to the right
tilting shot	the camera moves vertically, i.e. upwards or downwards
tracking shot	the camera follows a person or an object

5

(Anti-) social network: Media and friendship

(Anti-) social network: Media and friendship

B5 a) Watch extract 1 from B2 again and identify the cinematic devices.

b) Consider the cinematic devices and explain their respective function within the framework of the film. What do they tell you about the setting, what about the character and his feelings?

c) It may help you to work with a viewing grid:
- Divide the sequence into different parts and label them.
- Note down specific cinematic devices for each part. It is not necessary to note down every single change in camera position or camera angle, but some devices stand out and have an obvious function.

DVD

Viewing grid

scene	action/picture content	cinematic devices	function/effect/meaning
1 The thirsty student			
2 Out on the street			
3 On the campus			
4 Kirkland House	Mark running up stairs to door of "his" house/dorm	tilting up to name	high expectations, haven
5 "Home"		close-up/point-of-view shot of open fridge and beer	Mark needs some intoxication to get over his hurt feelings

B6 Use your notes to outline how the director uses cinematic devices to create an atmosphere of anticipation and to set the stage for the development of the plot, i.e. the creation of Facebook. This checklist will help you.

Checklist
Analyzing a film scene
- ✓ Remember to write a meaningful introduction to your analysis. Refer to the question.
- ✓ Don't present your findings in chronological order. Try to find groups of devices and explain them in context.
- ✓ Always identify a cinematic device with reference to the picture content and explain why it is used; e.g. "The director uses a close-up of Mark to show the character's feelings of frustration and pent-up humiliation."; "Point-of-view shots of the beer in the fridge and of the computer are used to reveal Mark's focus – these are the two things that will keep him company and help him get over his disappointment."
- ✓ Always provide an interpretation of the cinematic device you have spotted.
- ✓ Come to a meaningful conclusion that sums up your findings.

Language support: film

The director ...	▶	makes frequent/ occasional use of device x.		
The character(s) ... Their relationship ...	▶	is/are shown/ presented/...	▶	in a x shot by a panning/ tilting camera.
Device x ...	▶	is used ... is employed ...	▶	to reveal .../to expose ... to make clear .../to highlight ... to emphasize .../to underline ... to suggest .../to criticize ... to ridicule .../...

(Anti-) social network: Media and friendship

Comprehension

B7 Before starting work on Facebook, Mark Zuckerberg created a program called Facemash while studying at Harvard. Hacking into the university's databases, he retrieved the female students' photos and programmed Facemash in such a way that two random girls' photos were put side by side, asking the users to click on the girl who they thought looked better.

Watch extract 2 from "The Social Network" (8.34 min–13.52 min) and describe how Mark and his friends spend the evening compared to the students at the Phoenix Club House.

Analysis

Editing

B8 Read the info-box below and match the functions (1–4) with the types of editing (A–D):

1. e.g. to present two sides of the same plot development, to speed up the action, to give the viewer additional information
2. to explain why a character is in a particular situation or how a problem came about
3. to hint at what the characters may be about to experience and show the effects their present actions can have
4. to link two subsequent scenes more closely in a way that supports the plot-based connection

---

Info: Editing

Every film is composed of **shots**. The beginning and end of a shot are marked by **cuts**, i.e. the change from one image to another one. Shots can be very short or – if the camera films without any interruption – long. In modern films, there are often a lot of cuts so that shots that deal with the same part of the plot form a **sequence**.
The way shots are linked is referred to as **editing** or **montage**, which is usually done in a specific way to establish a meaningful relationship between the individual shots.
Typical examples of shots are:

types of editing	definition	function
A flashforward	a scene that shows what may happen in the future and thus interrupts the chronological order of the plot	
B flashback	a scene that shows what happened in the past and thus interrupts the chronological order of the plot	
C cross-cutting / parallel action	combining shots of two or more scenes which are usually taking place at the same time	
D match cut	two scenes that are connected by visual or acoustic means, e.g. a door is closed in one scene and opened in the following scene in a different context, someone is crying at the end of the first and the beginning of the second scene	

(Anti-) social network: Media and friendship

B9 a) Identify the kind of editing that is used in extract 2 from the film (8.34 min–13.52 min).

b) Explain its effect on the viewer.

B10 A film tells a story which means that it relies on narrative elements in addition to the cinematic devices employed.

a) Read the info-box and use the categories for your analysis of the film sequence in extract 2.

Info: Film – narrative elements
When analyzing film you should also study the following aspects:

- Setting: Determine the time and place of action.
- Plot: Watch what happens and try to understand the implications.
- Characters: Study the characters are presented by
  - their outward appearance (clothes / looks)
  - their body language (movements /gestures/ facial expression)
  - the way they speak.
- Character constellation: Note how different characters are related or interact.
- Objects: Give special consideration to specific objects (frequently shown in close-ups) which may have a key function or even a symbolic meaning.

These aspects may be especially important when contrasting two scenes.

---

b) Divide the class into two groups. One half of the class concentrates on what is going on in Mark's dorm, the other one on what is happening at the party at the Phoenix club. Concentrate on the editing and the points below (see info-box) and make notes in a grid:

aspect	function/effect
characters and character constellation:	
– …	
– …	

c) Compare your notes within your group and add what you have missed.

d) Form mixed groups with two experts from each side and present your findings to each other. Write down the key points of the other group.

e) Use your notes to analyze how cinematic devices and other techniques are used to combine and contrast what is going on in Mark's dorm and at the party.

5 (Anti-) social network: Media and friendship

Comment/Creative writing

B11 Read the article from *The Harvard Crimson*, the Harvard University's newspaper that reports on Facemash and the reactions to it. Write a letter to the editor in which you give your opinion on Facemash and the reactions to it.

Checklist: Letter to the editor p. 133

Hot or Not? Website Briefly Judges Looks

By **Bari M. Schwartz**, CONTRIBUTING WRITER   Published: Tuesday, November 04, 2003

Harvard students often compete in the classroom, but for at least a few hours this weekend, only one thing helped them make the grade—their looks.

[…] a website created by Mark E. Zuckerberg […] gave students a chance to rate their peers using ID photos taken from online House facebooks[1].

"Were we let in for our looks? No. Will we be judged on them? Yes," proclaimed the site, which Zuckerberg has now taken offline. Zuckerberg, a computer science concentrator[2], said he created the site – www.facemash.com – by hacking into House online facebooks and compiling ID photos onto his website, allowing viewers to vote for the "hotter" of two randomly chosen photos or rate the looks of students in a particular House against fellow-residents.

A link to the site was forwarded on many House and student group e-mail lists over the weekend—including the Institute of Politics (IOP), Fuerza Latina and the Association of Black Harvard Women (ABHW)—prompting both praise and criticism across campus.

But by Sunday night, outrage from individuals and student groups led Zuckerberg, who said he never expected such widespread publicity, to shut down the site for good[3].

By that time, Zuckerberg said, there had been 450 visitors to the site who had voted on their peers' photos at least 22,000 times.

"I don't see how it can go back online. Issues about violating people's privacy don't seem to be surmountable. The primary concern is hurting people's feelings," Zuckerberg said. "I'm not willing to risk insulting anyone."

Leyla R. Bravo '05, president of Fuerza Latina, said she sent a link to the website out over the group's e-mail list to let people know about what she viewed as a problem.

"I heard from a friend and I was kind of outraged," she said. "I thought people should be aware."

Both Fuerza Latina and ABHW received apology e-mails from Zuckerberg yesterday.

In the letter, Zuckerberg wrote that he was mainly interested in the computer science behind the venture.

"I understood that some parts were still a little sketchy[4] and I wanted some more time to think about whether or not this was really appropriate to release to the Harvard community," he wrote.

According to Zuckerberg, it was his intention to only show a few friends to get their opinion on the site, but someone forwarded the link to a friend and the chain of e-mails continued from there.

"When I returned from a meeting at around 10 p.m.," he wrote in the letter, "traffic was out of hand, and after thinking about the best course of action, I shut down the site around 10:30."

[1] **facebook** = Studenten-Jahrbuch
[2] **concentrator** = a student specializing in a field of study
[3] **for good** = permanently
[4] **sketchy** = not detailed or complete

Checklist: Creative writing pp. 128–129

B12 Imagine a girl/the boyfriend of a girl whose photo has been used on Facemash meets Mark Zuckerberg in a hallway. Write a dialogue in which the different views on the program are expressed.

(Anti-) social network: Media and friendship

Getting to the point

Comprehension

C1 Watch extract 3 (20.45 min–23.22 min) and outline what happens in the scene.

DVD

Analysis

C2 Analyze how cinematic devices are used to reveal the relationship between the characters involved.

Checklist: Text analysis p. 125

Comment

C3 As Zuckerberg was elected "Person of the Year" 2010, TIME devoted a long article to the man and his career. Compare the description of the Zuckerberg in the film as opposed to the Zuckerberg described in the extract from the article below. Judging on the basis of what you have learned about him in this theme discuss which version you would agree with.

Checklist: Comment pp. 126-127

[...] Zuckerberg's life at Harvard and after was the subject of a movie released in October called *The Social Network* [...]. [It] is a rich, dramatic portrait of a furious, socially handicapped genius who spits corrosive monologues in a monotone to hide his inner pain. This character bears almost no resemblance to the actual Mark Zuckerberg. [...]

Zuckerberg has often – possibly always – been described as remote and socially akward, but that's not quite right. [...] Zuckerberg is a warm presence, not a cold one. He has a quick smile and doesn't shy away from eye contact. He thinks fast and talks fast, but he wants you to keep up. He exudes not anger or social anxiety, but a weird calm. [...]

(TIME, by Lev Grossmann, 1/3/2011)

5 (Anti-) social network: Media and friendship

Speaking

Skills
How to analyze statistics
pp. 150-151

Skills
How to work with cartoons
p. 134

Skills
How to improve your oral skills
pp. 148-149

Skills
How to give feedback/peer-edit
pp. 144-145

D1 a) Roll a dice. Study the material on pages 81-82 that matches the number on your dice and work on the corresponding tasks.

⚀ ⚁ Statistics	⚂ ⚃ Cartoons	⚄ ⚅ Articles
1. Describe the graph.	1. Describe the cartoon.	1. Paraphrase the extract from the article in your own words.
2. Explain what it tells you about the way social networks like Facebook are used.	2. Explain what the cartoon makes fun of or criticizes about the use of social networks.	2. Compare what it says about social networks with your own experiences.

b) Group work: Present your findings to the group. Give each other feedback on your presentations.

Checklists

Statistics
✓ Say what type of graph it is (e.g. bar chart, pie chart).
✓ Say what the diagram is about.
✓ Describe the different elements of the diagram and how the figures are related to each other (e.g. if they increase/decrease over time).
✓ Draw conclusions from the figures.

Cartoons
✓ Describe both the text elements (e.g. caption, speech bubbles) and visual elements of the cartoon.
✓ Explain what real-life issue the cartoonist refers to and what his/her message is in that respect.

Articles
✓ Express the message of the extract in your own words.
✓ Use your personal experiences and background knowledge to comment on the message of the extract.

Checklist

Giving feedback – Presentations
✓ Was the presentation easy to follow (correct pronunciation, pauses where necessary, emphasis on important points, clear structure, correct use of language)?
✓ Did he/she use different and suitable words to describe the statistics/cartoon/article?
✓ Did he/she present his/her material confidently and competently?

(Anti-) social network: Media and friendship

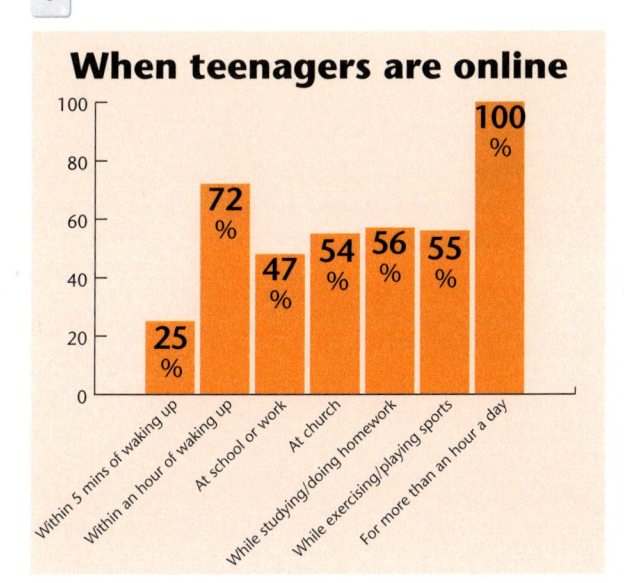

When teenagers are online

- Within 5 mins of waking up: 25%
- Within an hour of waking up: 72%
- At school or work: 47%
- At church: 54%
- While studying/doing homework: 56%
- While exercising/playing sports: 55%
- For more than an hour a day: 100%

What users dislike

- People sharing too much info about themselves: 36%
- Other posting things about you without asking permission: 36%
- Other people seeing posts you didn't mean them to see: 27%
- Temptation or pressure to share too much info about yourself: 24%
- Pressure to post content that will be popular and will get lots of comments/likes: 12%
- Pressure to comment on content posted by others in your network: 12%
- Seeing posts about social activities you weren't included in: 5%

AFTER ALL OUR ONLINE CHATS, I'M HAPPY TO FINALLY MEET YOU IN PERSON!

ME TOO!

"You have the right to remain silent. Anything you say may be used against you on Facebook, Twitter and YouTube!"

GLASBERGEN

(Anti-) social network: Media and friendship

⚄

1. Nobody actually wants to just read about what you're doing anymore.
Think about it: What sounds more appealing (and believable)? Reading a status that says, "I'm currently hanging out with Will Smith!" or a picture of that person actually posing with Smith? A photo is definitely more engaging. [...] When TIME interviewed teenagers about their social
5 media use in March, 16-year-old Hamp Briley explained that kids these days don't have time for Facebook: "Twitter's all statuses, Instagram's all pictures. People like to do more specific things like that instead of being on just Facebook."

(Renee Jacques, 11 Reasons to Quit Facebook in 2014, Huffington Post, 30 Dec 2013)

⚅

Two-thirds of the teenagers surveyed said people were "mostly kind" to each other on these networks, even as 88 percent said they had witnessed "people being mean or cruel." One in five admitted to having joined in on the cruelty.
Notably, one in five teens surveyed said they had been "bullied," but of those, the largest share
5 said they had been bullied in person, not online. Indeed, online and offline sentiments often merge: one in four said an online squabble resulted in a face-to-face argument or worse.
What do they do when they see or feel the brunt of cruelty online?
The vast majority say they ignore it. Girls are more likely to seek advice than boys. And when they do seek advice, teenagers are more likely to turn to their peers than their parents. Parents
10 are not entirely useless. The survey found that 86 percent of teens said parents advised them on "how to use the Internet responsibly and safely."

(Somini Sengupta, Teenagers Tell Researchers It's a Cruel, Cruel Online World, New York Times, 9 November 2011)

D2 a) In a discussion, your statements gain more credibility if you refer back to what others have said before you. The following phrases may help you do that. Sort them into the right categories below.

> I couldn't have said it better. – In spite of what you have just said, I still think ... – I see your point, but ... – What I'm trying to say is ... – To my mind ... – You may have a point there, but I still have some doubts about ... – Let me interrupt you for a second – That is definitely not the case. – You can say that again. – I know, but it isn't as simple as that. – I couldn't agree more. – The way I see it ... – Exactly! – Personally, I feel that ... – What I mean is ... – Look, it's like this: ... – Hang on a second. – That is just not right. – That's news to me. Where did you get that from? – That might be the case, but ... – That's not what I meant. I was just pointing out that ... – From my point of view ...

Agreeing	Disagreeing	Partly agreeing	Clarifying	Expressing your view	Interrupting

b) Add more phrases to the lists.

(Anti-) social network: **Media and friendship**

5

D3 In the second part of an oral exam, you are expected to discuss a topic. In order to prepare for the discussion, you will work on two sets of articles – set A and set B. You will use the information from the articles in a discussion – a task that is similar to the second part of an oral exam.

Skills
How to improve your oral skills
pp. 148-149

a) Pair work: Pick either set A or B of the articles (pp. 84-87). One of you reads and prepares article 1, the other article 2:
- Look up words you do not know.
- Identify the problem discussed in the article.
- Note down the evidence and arguments put forward in the article.

Skills
How to work with a dictionary
pp. 142-143

b) Group work: Form groups of four (one pair that focussed on set A and one pair that focussed on set B).
The pair with set A begins. The pair with set B listens to give feedback.
Follow these steps:
- Flip a coin – 'heads' for dialogue card 1, 'tails' for dialogue card 2.

Skills
How to give feedback/peer-edit
pp. 144-145

Set A – Dialogue card 1
Discuss whether ten years of Facebook has changed people's lives for the better.
Use arguments from your article and your own ideas.
Use the discussion phrases from D2.

Set A – Dialogue card 2
Discuss whether after ten years people have started to grow tired of Facebook.
Use arguments from your article and your own ideas.
Use the discussion phrases from D2.

- Begin your discussion.
- During the discussion, the other pair takes notes to give feedback afterwards. The checklist below may help you.
- Now it is the turn of pair B to have their discussion. Follow the steps above.

Set B – Dialogue card 1
Discuss whether Facebook is a virtual place in which it is good for teens to spend a lot of their free time.
Use arguments from your article and your own ideas.
Use the discussion phrases from D2.

Set B – Dialogue card 2
Discuss whether Facebook has to change to stay attractive and be accepted as a social network.
Use arguments from your article and your own ideas.
Use the discussion phrases from D2.

Checklist
Giving feedback – Dialogues
✓ Was the dialogue easy to follow (correct pronunciation, pauses where necessary, emphasis on important points, clear structure, correct use of language)?
✓ Did the students explain their point of view clearly, e.g. by using discussion phrases?
✓ Did they interact and refer to each other's arguments?

Articles Set A – (A1)

Hannah Slapper, Facebook: 10 years of trying to be liked (The Guardian, 3 February 2014)

It's the social media site's birthday. Time to face up to reality – I'm in love with the projection of my own desired life

I joined Facebook just before my 18th birthday, in 2007, so psychologically I associate my pre-FB life with childhood, and my post-FB life with adulthood.

The whole concept of Facebook perfectly spoons the student lifestyle. You can share your pretentious thoughts, upload your many #gpoy (that's gratuitous pictures of yourself) and basically shout about all your drinking, drug-taking and the French philosophy you're reading.
[...]

As any graduate will remember, those years at university were just as much about juggling a melee of friendships as it was about studying. Facebook allowed me to interact with Danny from my course as much as it allowed me to stalk/check out that potential psychopath I met on Tottenham Court Road, while organising birthday drinks with the girls from my halls. At the time I felt like master of my universe. In hindsight, I just look like the worst person in the universe. There are hundreds of pictures of me, mouth open, holding a bottle of sparkling wine, smiling with eyes-akimbo in the middle of Roxy. [...]

The comforting fact is that many of the people I know are in the same boat. They've turned into (vaguely) respectable adults who do not offend me with their internet behaviour, but lurking beneath their recently tagged holiday photos and refreshingly witty picture captions there are albums upon albums of evidence that they were, in fact, once 19 years old and an embarrassing person.

This is where it starts to get chilling. After a recent watch of Spike Jonze's Her, it suddenly dawned on me that sharing my life on this particular social media platform was an unquestioned and essential part of my life, just like breathing and eating. [...]

We've lived through so many of Facebook's design changes over the years, from mutual friends to "liking" pages, and from cover photos to the view-as feature. The most significant, however, has to be the timeline. Back in 2011, when this was being implemented, all we did was complain that it looked ugly, but the social implications of this redesign are enormous. Facebook had realised that people were using their platform to share the most significant moments of their life, and they needed a way to highlight this.

Got engaged? I bet you thought about how you were going to announce it. Had a baby? Chances are you were asked for pictures, and got an obscene amount of likes for posting photos of your new bundle of joy. [...]

Why do I, and millions of other people all over the world feel this need to compulsively share every moment of our lives in this carefully crafted way? [...] Facebook has created a new thing: lifestyleism. I'm guilty of it, as are all of you. I want people to think I'm a cool London writer, going out and being "in my 20s". I don't want people to know I sit on my bedroom floor on a Friday night and order two pizzas while watching Nothing To Declare and scrolling through Tinder. So I update my profile picture regularly, I choose a cover image that will make people laugh. I think carefully about my status updates and ensure they'll garner a few likes, maybe even a few comments.

Although I might not be quite ready for it now, I'm gradually realising that this needs to stop. How on earth am I going to become the person I want to be if it's this easy to trick everyone into thinking that I'm already there? I'm in love with an operating system, just like Spike Jonze imagined, but the object of my affections is the projection of my own desired life, and that is a more than enough reason to delete it forever [...].

Articles Set A – (A2)

Marco della Cava, How Facebook changed our lives (USA Today, 2 February, 2014)

The calendar may say 2014, but in tech culture this week actually marks the year 10 A.F — After Facebook.

What did we poor humans do before the advent of Mark Zuckerberg's collegiate brainstorm? Let's see, we smiled when we "liked" something, we dialed the phone to "update" friends and "tagging" was a kids' game. [...]

"The biggest impact of Facebook was that it broke us out of e-mail jail," says Paul Saffo, a longtime Silicon Valley futurist. "E-mail implied you had to reply, Facebook did not. E-mail is formal, Facebook is a salutation. E-mail you send, Facebook you broadcast. It's simply a new social medium for which we're still learning the social norms." [...]

Your childhood neighborhood may be but a memory, but it could gather once again on Facebook.

"In the recent past, if you left people physically for a job or marriage, you simply moved on, but Facebook made maintaining those relationships easy," says Danah Boyd of Microsoft Research and author of the forthcoming book, *It's Complicated: The Social Lives of Networked Teens*.

"The important takeaway from Facebook's rise is that people have a desire to connect broadly," she says. "For the longest time, technology limited communication to one on one; just think of the telephone. But now our worlds are complicated networks that overlap. The implications of that have yet to be fully realized."

[...]

"I lived in California and my grandmother lived in upper Michigan, and I had felt really badly about losing touch until she got a laptop and signed up for Facebook," says Kristy Campbell, 46, a communications director at Juniper Networks.

"Our world opened up to her. She attended my daughter's graduation and prom via Facebook, and when she suddenly passed away. I was left with a digital record of our interactions that I will never take down," says Campbell, who also used the site to create a network of divorcees that helped each other through that life change. "I really don't remember life before Facebook."

For every Facebook user who may have gotten tired of maintaining their page and quit, countless testimonials speak to the network's transformative effect.

Ann Friedlander, 65, of West Palm Beach, Fla., has children in Hong Kong, Connecticut and California. Without Facebook, she says, "I'd never know what they're up to or see photos of my grandchildren."

She also used the site to get back in touch with childhood friends in New Jersey and, more poignantly "discovered, through Facebook, that a neighbor died on 9/11 trying to rescue someone." [...]

And while much has been made of late about how younger generations are fast migrating away from Facebook to newer social networking sites and apps, Bella Maestas, 15, of Hillsborough, Calif., loves the way Facebook helps her tackle homework with classmates and stay connected socially.

"In a way, it takes the place of the diary," she says. "It also leaves a mark of you on the world. Everyone wants to be known, noticed and remembered." [...]

Facebook's willingness to be flexible with its approach when it has to be will be key to its future, says Bret Taylor, the company's former chief technology officer who oversaw integration with Apple's iOS software as well as the adoption of the famous Like button.

"Facebook could be very different in 10 years, but I see it being around, because it's not afraid to change often," he says, offering as example the company's purchase of photo-sharing site Instagram for $1 billion last April.

[...] Facebook's next decade is likely to be more tumultuous than its culturally dominant first 10 years. A recent YPulse survey revealed that 65% of those under 18 thought Facebook was "losing its cool factor." [...]

Articles Set B – (B1)

Jenna Wortham, Still on Facebook, but Finding Less to Like (NY Times, 16 November 2013)

Just a few years ago, most of my online social activity revolved around Facebook. I was an active member of several Facebook groups, [...]. And I used Facebook to stay up-to-date on the latest achievements of my sisters and their children, and the many members of my extended family.

But lately, my formerly hyperactive Facebook life has slowed to a crawl. I've found that most of my younger relatives have graduated from high school and have deleted their accounts or whittled them down until there is barely any personal information left. As for my own account, I rarely add photographs or post updates about what I've been doing. [...]

(T)his month, during a quarterly earnings call, David A. Ebersman, Facebook's chief financial officer, made a startling acknowledgment. Facebook had noticed "a decrease in daily users, specifically among younger teens," he said. Those teenagers, mostly American and likely around 13 or 14, weren't deleting their accounts, he said, but they were checking the site less often.

[...] And though Facebook is still the default social network for many people, perhaps it is no longer as crucial as it once was for social survival.

One explanation is that Facebook's function may now be different from what it was in its earlier days.

Nathan Jurgenson, a sociologist who studies the Internet [...], described mainstream social networking sites as "kind of like the mall." People mill about, peeking through windows into one another's lives, for lack of something better to do online. That is especially true for teenagers, he said.

[...]

S. Shyam Sundar, a director of the Media Effects Research Lab at Pennsylvania State University, said that Facebook had become a utility, like a phone carrier. People go to Facebook to document the major events in their lives, he said, and keep track of those of others, not unlike a public, community scrapbook.

[...] "It's a place where everyone is, that has a purpose and a place, but doesn't necessarily represent a place where people will want to go on a frequent basis."

In other words, as it has become nearly universal, Facebook may have lost some of its edge — or, at the very least, it may no longer feel novel or original to some of its users. It's possible that it has lost some of the cachet that made it appealing, especially for young users.

[...] Those cracks in Facebook's veneer have provided a market opening for other messaging services among young people in the United States and worldwide. Mr. Sundar calls those services — which include WhatsApp [...] — "mini social media," because they satisfy one desire among teenagers: keeping in constant communication.

"That is an aspect of being a teen — they love chatting with their friends and they are always on their phones," he said.

With the lightning speed at which social media is evolving, it is at least possible that Facebook is already entering a midlife crisis. Could we be approaching peak Facebook? The company is certainly paying attention to its footprint in the market — it bought Instagram, the popular photo-sharing service [...]

But if teenagers use Facebook less often, youth-oriented advertisers might spend less of their marketing budget on the site. And if teenagers are ultimately spending less time there, other users might follow suit, affecting the company's overall potential for moneymaking.

Facebook can manage very well without the support of teenagers, Mr. Sundar said. "But the truth is that teens are often the initial adopters," he said. "The real danger to Facebook might be the companies where they are going."

Articles Set B – (B2)

Perri Klass, Seeing Social Media More as Portal Than as Pitfall (NY Times, 9 January 2012)

More than a hundred years ago, when the telephone was introduced, there was some hand-wringing over the social dangers that this new technology posed: increased sexual aggression and damaged human relationships. [...]

In other words, the telephone provoked many of the same worries that more recently have been expressed about online social media. "When a new technology comes out that is something so important, there is this initial alarmist reaction," Dr. Moreno said.

Indeed, much of the early research [...] on social media seemed calculated to make parents terrified of an emerging technology that many of them did not understand as well as their children did.

Whether about sexting or online bullying or the specter of Internet addiction, "much social media research has been on what people call the danger paradigm," said Dr. Michael Rich, [...] the director of the Center on Media and Child Health at Children's Hospital Boston.

Though there are certainly real dangers, and though some adolescents appear to be particularly vulnerable, scientists are now turning to a more nuanced understanding of this new world. Many have started to approach social media as an integral, if risky, part of adolescence, perhaps not unlike driving.

Researchers are also looking to Facebook, Twitter and the rest for opportunities to identify problems, to hear cries for help and to provide information and support. Dr. Rich, who sees many teenagers who struggle with Internet-related issues, feels strongly that it is important to avoid blanket judgments about the dangers of going online. [...]

Going back and forth, as I do these days, between the worlds of academic pediatrics and academic journalism, I am struck by the focus in both settings on the potential — and the risks — of social media and on the importance of understanding how communication is changing.

Our children are using social media to accomplish the eternal goals of adolescent development, which include socializing with peers, investigating the world, trying on identities and establishing independence.

In 2011, the [...] clinical report, "The Impact of Social Media on Children, Adolescents and Families" [...] began by emphasizing the benefits of social media for children and adolescents, including enhanced communication skills and opportunities for social connections.

"A large part of this generation's social and emotional development is occurring while on the Internet and on cellphones," the report noted.

Our job as parents is to help them manage all this wisely, to understand — and avoid — some of the special dangers and consequences of making mistakes in these media. [...]

And both parents and researchers need to be sure they understand the subtleties of the ways teenagers interpret social media. [...] What adults interpret as bullying is often read by teenagers as "drama," a related but distinct phenomenon.

By understanding how teenagers think about harsh rhetoric, the researchers suggested, we may find ways to help them defend themselves against the real dangers of online aggression.

The problems of cyberbullying and Internet overuse are serious, and the risks of making mistakes online are very real. But even those who treat adolescents with these problems are now committed to the idea that there are other important perspectives for researchers — or parents, or teachers — looking at the brave new universe in which adolescence is taking place.

Social media, said Dr. Rich, "are the new landscape, the new environment in which kids are sorting through the process of becoming autonomous adults — the same things that have been going on since the earth cooled."

6 A question of gender

Getting started

A1 a) Study the two photos and tell your partner your immediate reaction.

b) Discuss the significance of the words "but" and "still" in the second picture.

c) Explain the connection between the facial expressions and posture of the three teenagers and the message expressed in the sentence.

d) In groups of three – one pupil for each person in the photographs – speak the sentence aloud expressing different emotions: anger, fear, boredom, humour, and passion.

A2 a) Read the extract from "Citizenship" by Mark Ravenhill quietly first.

b) Divide into five groups: Find a partner within your group. Each group practises reading the lines in a different way. Group 1: angry, group 2: frightened, group 3: bored, group 4: giggly, group 5: passionate

c) One pair from each group presents their version to the class.

d) Discuss the different effects created by your dramatic readings and decide on the most appropriate version.

Extract from "Citizenship" by Mark Ravenhill

[…]
Tom   You're alright. You're a good person. I like you.
Amy   Yeah?
5 Tom   I really like you.
Amy   Thass good.
Tom   You got a nice face.

Amy kisses Tom.
Oh.
10 Amy   Was that wrong?
Tom   I didn't mean you to do that.
Amy   Oh. Right. Right.
Tom   I didn't wanna kiss you.
15   Only –
Amy   Yeah?
Tom   I'm not ready for –
Amy   You're fifteen.
Tom   I know.
Amy   You gotta have done.
20 Tom   No.
Amy   Why?
Tom   It doesn't matter.
Amy   Tell me.
Tom   I have this dream. And
25   in this dream I'm
  kissing someone. Real
  kissing. Tongues and
  that. But I can't see
  who I'm kissing. I don't
30   know if it's a woman.
  Or a man. I try to see
  the face. But I can't.
Amy   Are you gay?
Tom   I don't know.
35 Amy   There's bisexual.
Tom   You won't tell anyone?
Amy   No. Are you going to decide?
Tom   What?
40 Amy   What you are?
Tom   I don't know.
Amy   Or find out?
Tom   I don't know.
Amy   Don't waste yourself,
45   Tom. You've got a nice face.
Tom   Yeah.
[…]

A question of gender: **Sexual identity**

6

Understanding the characters

A3 a) Find a partner who had the same role as you in A2 (Amy or Tom). Go through your character's lines and discuss what the character might actually be thinking while speaking those lines. Write down his or her thoughts.

b) Find another pair who wrote down the thoughts of the other character.

- Amy and Tom should be sitting next to each other while the persons with their "thoughts" could stand behind them.
- Amy and Tom: Read your lines slowly to each other.
- Amy and Tom's thoughts: Read out Amy and Tom's thoughts that go with their spoken lines.

c) In your group discuss to what extent adding the characters' thoughts helps you understand them.

Staging a play

A4 a) Amy and Tom talk about intimate things like their sexual orientation. If you had to stage this particular scene, what kind of setting and scenery would you choose? In groups of four discuss your ideas and come to a decision about:

- setting
- props
- lighting effects
- scenery/stage design
- costumes
- sound effects

Language support: expressing your ideas
These sentence beginnings can help you express your ideas: • If I were the director, … • If I had to stage the play, … • The setting should take into account … • The scenery could reflect … • I suggest that the costumes … • My idea would be to include pauses and silences because … • I would choose the following props to underline …

Language support: drama terms
• cast/dramatist • playwright/director • script • stage directions • stage design/scenery/props/lighting effects/sound effects/volume • pauses/silences • dialogue/monologue • gestures/facial expressions • scene • to stage a play • to perform a role • to cast so. in a role

b) Compare your ideas in class.

6 A question of gender: Sexual identity

Practice section

Pre-reading

B1 a) Think-pair-share: In what contexts and in what ways is sexuality or sexual identity a subject you talk about
- at school?
- in private outside school?

b) Explain to what extent the two different settings have an impact on the ways sexuality is discussed.

Comprehension

B2 a) Read the extract from "A Vampire Story" by Moira Buffini.

b) In groups of seven create a freeze frame that visualizes the scene. In order to be able to do that you first have to discuss aspects such as the relationships between the characters or the atmosphere.

c) Present your freeze frames to the other groups. Let the audience first describe who and what they see. Then explain your intentions.

d) Decide which freeze frame best captures the scene.

This Extract from Moira Buffini's play "A Vampire Story" is set during the first drama lesson in the new school year. Mint is the drama teacher. All other characters are his students: Frank, Briggs and Moon are schoolboys; Debit, Point, and Ella/Eleanor are schoolgirls.

Frank has sensitive eyes and a nervous demeanour[1]. Mint is full of fervour[2] and frustration. Mint's students, Briggs, Point, Debit and Moon, have perfected an air of cultivated
5 *boredom. They look as if they haven't had any fresh air in years. They look in fact, like detached, fashionable, effortlessly nonchalant vampires.*
[...]
Mint So, same old spoilt rebels and fashion
10 victims as last year. Not allowed to swear with disappointment or I would. Briggs
Briggs Mint
Mint I'm gutted[3] to see you; I thought you'd be shovelling fries for the rest of your life.
15 And Debit
Debit Hello, Mint
Mint You actually passed an exam?
Debit Might have
Mint So there's a brain somewhere under all
20 that hair spray

Debit It's mousse
Mint Well, let's see how long you last
Point No, Mint, why don't we see how long you last?
25 **Mint** We're off to a great start already. Now, I'm more than delighted to see that we have some new blood. What are your names?
Ella Eleanor Wythenshawe
Mint And?
30 **Frank** Frank Adam Stein
Mint OK, Ella and – one name will do – Frank. I'm going to throw you in at the deep end. What's the first rule of making drama? Come on! First rule of making drama?
35 **Debit** Just say 'Yes'
Mint Thank you, Debit. 'Yes'. Yes to an idea, yes to each other, yes to the energy, to the communal experience, yes to the mighty, universal 'yes'. That's what we aspire to in
40 this class, isn't it?

[1] **demeanour** = the way a person behaves towards others
[2] **fervour** = very strong feeling or enthusiasm
[3] **to be gutted** = to be disappointed

A question of gender: Sexual identity

Moon No
Mint So. The hot seat[4]. Frank – let's start with you
Frank What?

Mint takes Frank to a seat apart from the group.

Mint We're going to put you on the hot seat
Frank What for? Why?
Briggs To scald[5] your arse
Mint The hot seat, guys, is a place of discovery, OK? Now we usually use it when we're 'in character', but I'm going to do something we've never tried before. I'm an instinctive teacher and my instincts are saying, 'Go, Mint, go.' So I'm going to throw away the code of good practice and hot seat you as yourself
Moon That's psychological torture, Mint
Mint It's going to be fun, OK?
Moon You could leave him permanently scarred
Mint Frank, the rest of the group will ask you questions
Moon You're infringing his human rights
Mint And your only job is to be truthful
Moon These are torture chamber conditions
Mint It's a simple question and answer exercise. Are you being tortured, Frank?
Frank Um
Mint Now, think about everything that has brought you to this moment in time. People, when I clap my hands we're going to begin – so have your questions for Frank ready

Frank is full of dread. Mint claps.

Moon Do you feel that in doing this, Mint is infringing your human rights?
Frank Um
Briggs What's your name?
Frank I've already said it
Briggs I didn't listen
Frank Frank
Briggs Frank what?
Frank Stein
Briggs What's that short for?
Frank Franklin
Moon Your name's Franklinstein?
Briggs *(laughing)* Are you lying?
Frank My dad thought it was funny too. In fact, it was his last big joke before his sense of humour calcified[6] and had to be removed
Point Are you a monster?
Frank Probably
Briggs Are you a wanker[7]?
Mint Briggs!
Debit What school were you at before, Franklin?
Frank I'm home-educated
Debit What?
Frank My mum and dad have been teaching me at home
Briggs How long for?
Frank Since I was a foetus
Moon You've never been to school?
Frank No
Point Why not?
Frank You'll have to ask my parents that really
Point No thanks
Frank Perhaps they were worried that I might grow up normal if I went to school so they decided to concentrate all their efforts on turning me into a freak
Point Why?
Frank Well, they're freaks, so I expect they just wanted me to fit in
Mint Frank, I can understand your defensiveness, but just try to be open. Say yes
Frank Well, to be fair on my mum and dad – that's Tina and Geoff – I think they had high hopes. They wanted me to fulfil my potential
Point What potential is that, Franklin?
Frank Tina and Geoff thought that if I learnt everything there is to know by the age of sixteen I might turn out to be a leader of men or a genius or something but I eventually had to point out the flaw in their plan and say, 'Tina and Geoff, if you don't let me go to school and talk to some other people, I'll end up in a nut house[8] before I'm twenty,' and to drive home[9] my point I painted my bedroom black and drowned Tina's pot plants so, given that I've got four 'A's at A Level already, they decided to let me come. They see it as a bit of a gap year, I think
Moon Did you say you were a genius?
Frank No, I'm a great disappointment
Briggs Are you gay?
Mint Question not allowed

---

[4] **hot seat** = the person in role is questioned or interviewed by other students and answers questions as that character.
[5] **to scald** = to burn with hot liquid or steam
[6] **to calcify** = to become hard, inflexible or unchanging
[7] **wanker** *(offensive sl)* = a stupid or unpleasant person; so. who masturbates
[8] **nut house** = an institution for the mentally ill
[9] **to drive home** = make clear by special emphasis and try to convince so. of sth.

A question of gender: Sexual identity

Moon Is God a man or a woman?
Frank Pardon?
Mint I think he means are you religious?
140 **Moon** No, is God a man or a woman?
Frank Um, if there was a deity or creator I'd say it would be unlikely to have recognisable genitalia.
Debit That's rude
145 **Frank** God probably transcends gender. The deity is probably asexual or even polysexual
Point Is that what you are, Frank?
Frank It may even be formless, dare I say it, non-existent and therefore imaginable in
150 any form
Debit I think you're shy about sex
Frank Is that a question?
Debit That's cute. You got any diseases?
Mint Not allowed
155 **Debit** Have you got a girlfriend, Frank?
Frank No
Briggs Have you got any friends at all?
Frank Yes, no, well, it depends what you mean by friends. If you mean actual living
160 people who like me, then no
Debit That's a bit sad, isn't it?
Frank I used to have an imaginary friend, but he moved out. He was great; really funny; much more daring than me. He used to
165 subvert Geoff's quizzes and put lighted matches in the bin, but in the end he had to go

Moon Why?
Frank It turned out he was hiding
170 pornography under the bed and Tina found it. She had a massive row with him. He came in to tell me he was leaving and I haven't seen him since
Ella Do you miss him?
175 **Frank** Yes
Debit So what d'you do for fun, Frank?
Frank Fun?
Moon Apart from the pornography
Frank That wasn't mine; it was imaginary
180 **Mint** One last question: what made you choose Drama, Frank?
Frank Um, my parents think it's a totally useless subject so it seemed like the obvious choice
185 **Mint** OK. Well done. Respect. Round of applause

Only Mint and Ella clap.

Briggs Frank
Frank Yes?
190 **Briggs** I love you

Frank flinches as if he's about to be hit.

[...]

B3 Read the info-box and explain the following quotation: "The text of a play is like the score of a symphony – a finished work, yet only a potentiality until it is performed". Consider what you have already learned in sections A and B to bring a play to life.

> **Info: Drama**
> Unlike novels or short stories, plays are not written to be read but to be performed on stage. A play is no more than a script that has to be brought to life as it only contains the dialogue and some stage directions. The recipient is directly confronted with the characters as there is no narrator who explains or interprets characters and situations. Consequently, plays are open to diverging interpretations.

A question of gender: Sexual identity

Analysis

B4 a) Mint decides to let Frank be himself on the hot seat. Describe and explain the students' reaction to Mint's decision.
In order to do this task consider the following aspects:
- **Dialogue:** Which students show any reaction to Mint's decision?
  → Only Moon, he calls Mint's decision "psychological torture" (l. 57).
  What else does he say and what does it reveal about his opinion of Mint's decision?
- **Stage directions:** What do the stage directions reveal about the students' reaction?
  → As Moon is the only student who protests against Mint's decision, what do the stage directions reveal about the other students' reactions?

b) Analyze how the language of both Mint and his students creates atmosphere.
In order to do this task find answers to the following questions:
- **Dialogue: What does the choice of words indicate?**
  → Mint: He uses deprecating words for his students, for example "spoilt rebels and fashion victims" (ll. 9–10). This indicates that Mint is rather disrespectful of his students. Find more examples.
  → His students: Point, for example, expresses doubts about Mint's future at the school: "No, Mint, why don't we see how long you last?" (ll. 23–24). Again, mutual disrespect becomes obvious.
  What is the nature of the dialogue?
  → The dialogue takes place during a drama lesson at school. The students demonstrate their lack of motivation while the teacher resorts to irony when he says "We're off to a great start already" (l. 25). Find other examples in which language contributes towards creating atmosphere in the classroom.
- **Pace:** What is the pace of this extract?
  → As the dialogue predominantly consists of rather short questions and equally short replies, the pace is quite fast in this extract.

Skills
Checklist:
Text analysis
p. 125

Language support: analyzing atmosphere	Language support: useful adjectives
The atmosphere can be described as … A hostile/relaxed/tense atmosphere is created by … The pace of the extract suggests that the atmosphere is … The prevailing atmosphere is … The … creates an atmosphere of …. The atmosphere evokes feelings of …/fits in with …/ foreshadows …/creates suspense …	positive: enjoyable, peaceful, calm, lively, comfortable, cheerful, relaxed, pleasant, harmonious, idyllic, picturesque, familiar, friendly, warm negative: grave, tense, unpleasant, disagreeable, dark, gloomy, dismal, dreary, depressing, desolate, discouraging, hopeless, cheerless, bleak

A question of gender: Sexual identity

> **Checklist**
> *Analyzing drama*
> When analyzing the script of a play, only the **dialogue** and possibly some **stage directions** offer answers to questions that help interpret and eventually produce the play. However, it's also important to pay attention to the following:
>
> ✓ **Plot and plot structure:** What happens in the play? What is the structure of the play? What techniques does the playwright use?
> ✓ **Themes:** What ideas are expressed in the play? What does the playwright tell us about the world and ourselves?
> ✓ **Characters:** Who are the characters in the play? What do they do? How do they feel? What conflicts are there? What are their relationships? What are their personal traits?
> ✓ **Setting:** What is the world of the play? Where does it happen? When does it happen?
> ✓ **Language in dialogues or monologues:** What does the choice of words indicate? What is the context and the nature of the dialogue? How are allusions and imagery used?
> ✓ **Pace:** What is the pace of the scene/play?
> ✓ **Atmosphere:** How is atmosphere created? How does the interaction of the characters/the language/the setting contribute to the atmosphere?

Comment/Creative writing

B5 Comment on Mint's understanding of his professional role as a drama teacher. Take into consideration his relationship to his students.

Checklist: Comment pp. 126-127

B6 Continue the dialogue: Now Moon is in the hot seat and his classmates ask him questions. In order to do this task consider the following aspects:

- **Characters:** Study Moon's role in the extract and identify his personal traits.
- **Themes:** Decide what Moon's classmates might want to find out about him.
- **Language:** Choose appropriate language (register, choice of words) for the students as well as for Mint.
- Include **stage directions** that indicate how the characters should behave.

Checklist: Creative writing pp. 128-129

A question of gender: Sexual identity

Getting to the point

Comprehension

C1 Read the extract from "Citizenship" by Mark Ravenhill below. Briefly summarize the extract and describe the different interests of the two characters.

Checklist: Summary p. 124

Analysis

C2 Analyze the dialogue between Tom and de Clerk and explain the means the playwright uses to create atmosphere.

Checklist: Text analysis p. 125

Comment/Creative writing

C3 Comment on the advice de Clerk gives to Tom at the end of the extract (ll. 131–139).

Checklist: Comment pp. 126-127

C4 Add a scene: Although Tom has still not talked to anyone who is homosexual, he has taken De Clerk's advice and decided to come out at school and make public that he is gay. Despite some neutral and even positive reactions of some of his classmates, Tom is seriously bullied by others and, consequently, desperate for help and support. He talks to his teacher De Clerk again. Write their dialogue and include appropriate stage directions.

Checklist: Creative writing pp. 128-129

> **Checklist**
> *Creative writing*
> ✓ Use information from the extract as a basis for a plausible dialogue.
> ✓ Stay in line with the characters' personal traits, the plot and atmosphere.
> ✓ Choose appropriate language (register, choice of words) for Tom and De Clerk.
> ✓ Include stage directions that indicate how the characters behave.

The following **Extract** is again taken from Mark Ravenhill's play "Citizenship" and set at school: Tom has made a mess of his coursework because he got some blood on it from a minor injury. He now has to rewrite it to make it look neat again. Mr de Clerk is his highly stressed teacher.

[...]
De Clerk's mobile rings.

Tom You gonna get that, sir?
De Clerk No.

5 *Mobile stops.*

Tom Might have been important.
De Clerk Nothing else matters. Nothing else matters but your coursework and the inspectors and that we don't become a
10 failing school, okay? There is nothing else in the whole wide world that matters apart from that.

Mobile rings again.

Tom They don't think so.
15 **De Clerk** Well fuck 'em, fuck 'em, fuck 'em.
Tom They really want to talk to you.
De Clerk Uhhh. *(Answers the mobile.)* No. Still at – I told you. I told you – because we've got the inspectors. No. No. Well put it in the
20 fridge and I'll … put it in the bin. I don't care. I don't care. I can't.
De Clerk ends the call.
Tom Are you married, sir?
De Clerk I'm not talking any more.
25 **Tom** I was just wondering.

De Clerk Well, don't.
Tom Other teachers say: my wife this or my girlfriend that. But you never do.
De Clerk Well, that's up to them.
30 **Tom** It makes you wonder. We all wonder.
De Clerk Listen, I'm here from eight in the morning until eight in the evening, midnight the last few weeks – maybe I don't have a personal life.
35 **Tom** Yeah.
De Clerk Maybe I'm not a person at all. Maybe I'm just lesson plans and marking.
Tom Yeah. Maybe.
De Clerk Oh. My head. Have you got a
40   Nurofen[1]?
Tom Sorry, sir?
De Clerk Have you got a Nurofen or something?
Tom No, sir. I had some but I took them all.
45 **De Clerk** Right.
Tom If you want to go home – go home to your ... partner.
De Clerk I can't.
Tom I can do a massage, sir. I know how to do
50   a massage.
De Clerk No.
Tom It stops headaches. I done it loads of times.
De Clerk Listen. Physical contact is –
55 **Tom** Out of lessons now.
De Clerk Difficult.
Tom Sssssssshhhh. Our secret.

Tom moves over to de Clerk and massages his shoulders and neck.

60 You've got to breathe too. Remember to keep breathing.
De Clerk Mmm.
Tom There's a lot of stress about, isn't there?
De Clerk It's all stress.
65 **Tom** How old are you?
De Clerk Twenty-two.
Tom Lots of teachers burn out before they're twenty-five because of all the stress.
De Clerk Mmm.
70 **Tom** You're quite developed, sir. Do you go to the gym?
De Clerk Sometimes.
Tom With your ... partner.

De Clerk Back to your work now. That was
75   wrong. Physical contact.
Tom Sir – I'm really sorry, but I've –

Tom wipes de Clerk's shoulder.

I've dripped on you, sir.
De Clerk What?
80 **Tom** You've got blood on your shirt.
De Clerk Oh, fuck.
Tom I'm really sorry. It's a really nice shirt.
De Clerk Shit. Shit. Shit.

De Clerk scrubs at his shoulder.

85 **Tom** If you want me to get you another one, sir –
De Clerk No no.
Tom I get a discount. My brother manages Top Man[2].
90 **De Clerk** Tom – get on with your work. You get on with your work and I'll get on with my work.
Tom You've got good clothes, sir. For a teacher.
De Clerk Tom.

95 *Pause.*

Tom Sir ... I keep on having this dream and in this dream I'm being kissed.
De Clerk Don't.
Tom Only I never know whether it's a man or
100   woman whose doing the kissing.
De Clerk This isn't Biology. I'm Citizenship.
Tom I think I dream about being kissed by a man.
De Clerk I don't want to know about that.
105 **Tom** I really want to know: do I dream about a man kissing me?
De Clerk Please. Don't do this. I'm tired. I'm exhausted. I've got the Head of Department chasing me. I've got the inspectors coming
110   after me like wolves after blood. I've still got eight hours of paperwork and I've done a full day's teaching. Please understand the pressure I'm under and just copy the work.
Tom What do you do if you're gay, sir?
115 **De Clerk** You talk to someone.
Tom I'm trying to talk to you.

---

[1] **Nurofen** = brand name of a range of pain-relief medication
[2] **Top Man** = a clothing store for men

De Clerk You don't talk to me. Talk to your form tutor.

Tom He hates me.

120 **De Clerk** I don't think so.

Tom What do you do at the weekends, sir?

De Clerk Alright. Go away. Go home.

Tom What about the coursework?

De Clerk I'll explain the blood to the
125 inspectors.

Tom Alright then.

Tom packs up his bag.

Bye then, sir.

De Clerk Bye, Tom.

130 **Tom** I want to talk to someone gay, sir. I don't know any.

De Clerk Shut up, please shut up.

Tom I really want to meet someone gay and ask them what it's like.

135 **De Clerk** Well – it's fine. It's normal. It's just fine.

Tom You reckon?

De Clerk You know the school policy: we celebrate difference. You report bullies.
140 Everything's okay. You're okay.

Tom I don't feel okay.

De Clerk Well – you should do.

[…]

Listening

Pre-listening

D1 Pair work:
  a) Tell each other what you know about the church's (Protestant and/or Catholic) attitude towards homosexuality and what you think the church's attitude towards homosexuality should be.

  b) Talk about whether schools should have anti-discriminatory rules with regard to sexual identity. Find arguments for and against possible rules.

  c) Read the short introduction to the Stateside-podcast "The Living Room: Identity and acceptance in West Michigan's LGBT community" and speculate about what Rachel Gleason might have experienced.

4:45 pm, Mon March 10, 2014

The Living Room: Identity and acceptance in West Michigan's LGBT community

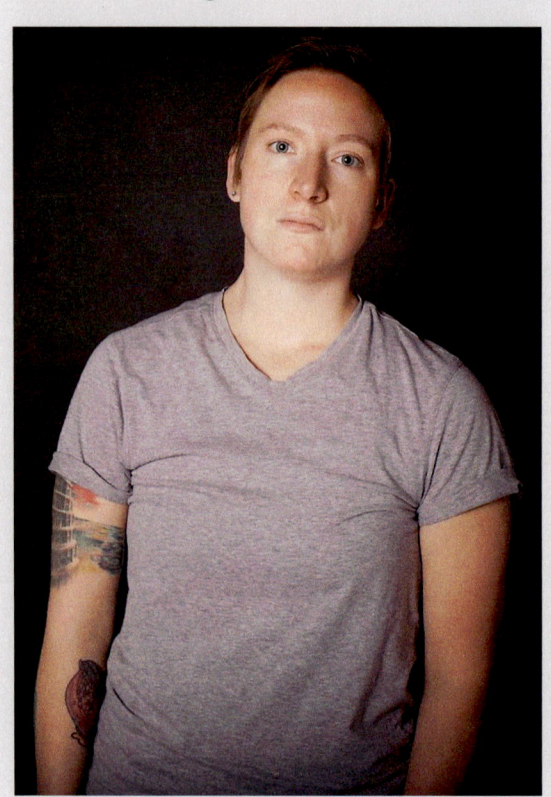

The Living Room is our ongoing storytelling series.

This story is the first in our series about identity and acceptance in West Michigan's LGBT (Lesbian, Gay, Bisexual, Transgender) community.

Rachel Gleason spent much of her youth at her church: worshipping, studying, singing, babysitting.

The church was her life. But that began to change when Rachel started to understand who she really was.

A question of gender: Sexual identity

While-listening

D2 a) Listen to the first few minutes (up to 4:21) of the podcast and make notes on information you get about Rachel Gleason and her church life.

b) Listen to the rest of the programme and put the following stages describing Rachel's coming-out into the correct order:

1. At college she writes her coming-out paper "My closet has a window".

2. Rachel has to make a decision: stay and pray and never get married or run away.

3. She starts to read gay literature.

4. Rachel feels humiliated.

5. Her friends turn away from her.

6. She is at peace with herself but still has nightmares about church.

7. Her mother finds her books; Rachel agrees to have counselling "to pray the gay away".

8. She decides to come out and not go to church anymore.

9. The pastors ban her from certain church duties until she is "healed".

10. She can't forgive the pastors at her former church.

DVD

Skills
How to listen effectively
p. 152

Post-listening

D3 a) Write down one word for each of the people that best describes their reaction to Rachel's coming out: her church and high school friends, her mother, her pastors, her professor.

b) Compare your words with a partner and give reasons for your choices.

D4 Group work (4): Talk to each other about:
- what you think of Rachel's story
- what you think of people's reactions to her coming out
- whether you know of institutions around you that might discriminate against homosexual people.

Listening and writing

D5 Use Rachel's story as an example and write a speech to be delivered to your school board in which you promote the implementation of an anti-discriminatory sexual identity policy for your school.

Skills
Checklist: Speech
p. 132

7 A (brave) new world

Getting started

A1 a) Express your personal vision of the future by writing an acrostic poem.
You may use the letters as initials but you can also place them in the middle of a word or a sentence.

b) Read at least four of your classmates' acrostics and decide which one you find most interesting. In class name your favourite ones and give reasons for your choice.

c) Present and discuss the poems that were chosen. Find similarities and differences between the various visions.

F
U
T
U
R
E

A2 a) Pair work: Study the figures and talk about the impact they might have on our future.

- 81.3% of Americans use the Internet, but only 16.1% of the people living in Africa do.
- $\frac{1}{3}$ of all websites are pornographic.
- 9% of people in the world own a car.
- One in six people have no access to clean water and almost 2.5 billion do not have access to adequate sanitation.
- Between 1.3 and 2.1 billion people are deprived of essential medicines.

b) Placemat (4): Note down five features which characterize a just, fair and generally positive future for you. Then agree on the three most important features for your group.

c) Compare your results in class.

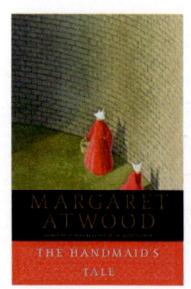

The Handmaid's Tale by Margaret Atwood (1985)
Atwood's novel, a chilling tale of a concubine in a patriarchal, oppressive future America, is more vital than ever. The Republic of Gilead, a tyrannical Christian fundamentalist society, allows the protagonist, Offred, only one function, namely to breed, in order to compensate the declining birth rates in a state ravaged by nuclear war and pollution. If she refuses to conform, she will, like all dissenters, be hanged at the wall or sent away to die slowly of radiation sickness.

Never Let Me Go by Kazuo Ishiguro (2005)
In his dystopian science fiction novel Kazuo Ishiguro presents the lives of a group of students growing up in a sinister version of contemporary England. "Never Let Me Go" hauntingly dramatizes their attempts to come to terms with their childhood at the seemingly idyllic Hailsham School. The fate that awaits the protagonist, Kathy, and her closest friends in the wider world is to provide organs as transplants for sick members of the ruling elite. For this purpose they have been specifically cloned to fulfil their role as donors.

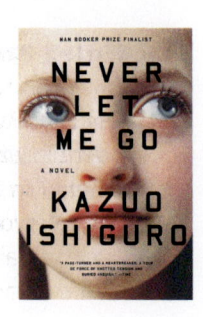

A (brave) new world: What will the future bring?

A3 a) Study the short descriptions of the novels below (pp. 100-101) and say how these books depict the future.

settings
e.g. tyrannical Christian fundamentalist society

environmental factors
e.g. nuclear radiation

Visions of the future

social groups/society
e.g. the ruling elite

consequences for mankind
e.g. declining birth rate

b) Complete the word web with words and phrases from the texts.

c) Compare the fictional visions with your own ideas (A1c and A2c) and identify common features.

A4 a) Read the info-box and decide whether the novels fit the definition of a dystopia.

b) Speculate and discuss why most fictional visions of the future tend to be dystopian rather than utopian.

Info: dystopia
The word **utopia** is a combination of the two Greek words "outopia" (no place) and eutopia (good place). The 16th century humanist, Sir Thomas More, called his fictional vision of an ideal imaginary society "Utopia". As a result, the literary term utopia is used to denote a work of fiction which depicts an ideal political state and way of life often set in the future. **Dystopia** ("bad place") is the opposite of utopia. The literary term dystopia refers to a type of fiction which represents a very unpleasant, undesirable or frightening imaginary world. Environmental, political, social or technological threats to our present society are often projected into the future as a warning in order to draw attention to real-world issues.

Gone by Michael Grant (2008-2013)
Michael Grant's breath-taking, dystopian, sci-fi saga "Gone" is a page-turning thriller. In the blink of an eye, everyone disappears. Gone. Except for the young. There are teens, but not one single adult. Just as suddenly, there are no phones, no Internet, no television. No way to get help. And no way to figure out what has happened. Hunger threatens. Bullies rule. A sinister creature lurks. Animals are mutating. And the teens themselves are changing, developing new talents—unimaginable, dangerous, deadly powers—that grow stronger by the day. It's a terrifying and disturbing new world.

The Circle by Dave Eggers (2013)
The time is somewhere in the not-too-distant future. The novel explores the frontiers of social media, looking forward not to a world of open potential, but to an encroaching nightmare. The company, the Circle, demands transparency in all things. Anonymity is banished; everyone's past is revealed; everyone's present may be broadcast live in video and sound. The Circle's goal is to have all aspects of human existence—from voting to love affairs—flow through its portal, the only such portal in the world.

7 A (brave) new world: What will the future bring?

Practice section

Pre-reading

B1 a) Group work (3): Tell each other whether you know the novel or the film and say what you think makes it is so popular.
b) Compare your ideas with those of another group.

Comprehension

B2 Read this extract from "The Hunger Games" by Suzanne Collins and talk to your partner about what event is taking place.

Extract 1 from "The Hunger Games" by Suzanne Collins

At one o'clock, we head for the square. Attendance is mandatory unless you are on death's door[1]. This evening, officials will come around and check to see if this is the case. If not,
5 you'll be imprisoned.

It's too bad, really, but they hold reaping in the square – one of the few places in District 12 that can be pleasant. The square's surrounded by shops, and on public market days, especially if
10 there is good weather, it has a holiday feeling to it. But today, despite the bright banners hanging on the buildings, there's an air of grimness. The camera crews, perched like buzzards on the rooftops, only add to the effect.
15 People file in silently and sign in. The reaping is a good opportunity for the Capitol to keep tabs on the population as well. Twelve to eighteen-year-olds are herded into roped areas marked off by ages, the oldest in front, the
20 young ones, like Prim, towards the back. Family members line up around the perimeter holding tightly to one another's hands. But there are others, too, who have no one they love at stake, or who no longer care, who slip among the
25 crowd taking bets on the two kids whose names will be drawn.

Odds are given[2] on their ages, whether they're Seam[3] or merchant[4], if they will break down and weep. Most refuse dealing with the racketeers, but carefully, carefully. These same people tend
30 to be informers, and who hasn't broken the law? I could be shot on a daily basis for hunting, but the appetites of those in charge protect me. Not everyone can claim the same.

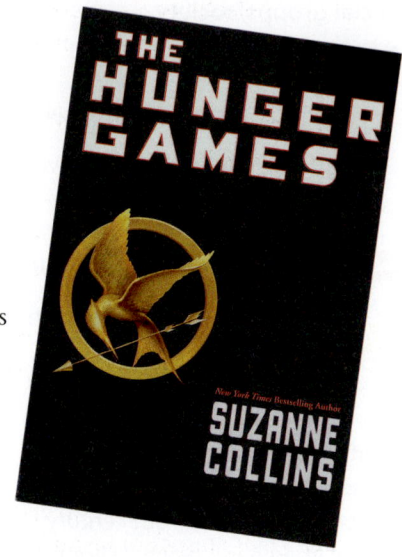

Anyway Gal and I agree that if we have to
35 choose between dying of hunger and a bullet in the head, the bullet would be much quicker.

The space gets tighter, more claustrophobic, as people arrive. The square's quite large, but not
40 enough to hold District 12's population of about eight thousand. Latecomers are directed to the adjacent streets, where they can watch the event on screens as it's televised by the state.

---

[1] **to be on death's door** = to be very ill and likely to die soon
[2] **odds are given** = *here*: people are able to bet on the chances of sth. happening
[3] **the Seam** = the nickname for the poorest section of District 12
[4] **merchant section** = area of District 12 which is wealthier than the Seam

A (brave) new world: What will the future bring? **7**

Analysis

Analyzing atmosphere

B3 a) Choose the most appropriate adjectives from the list below to describe the atmosphere in extract 1.

> exciting – foreboding – relaxed – emotional – light-hearted – electrifying – menacing – unremarkable – sinister – thrilling – exhilarating – ominous – captivating – high-spirited – peaceful

b) Find appropriate sentences in the extract to support and explain your choice of adjectives.

Example: *The sentence on line … illustrates a menacing atmosphere because …*
The sentence on line … shows/reveals/exemplifies the foreboding atmosphere in this scene because …

B4 To explore the atmosphere of a fictional text more closely you should take the following aspects into consideration:

- choice of **setting**
- use of **language**

Settings are important to evoke an appropriate mood or atmosphere for particular episodes in a novel.

a) Read extract 1 again and note down what you find out about its setting. In doing so take into account:

- how the setting is described

  Example: *The extract is set in a very large square, which is capable of holding several thousand people. Despite the size of the square there is not enough room for everyone (cf. lines 39 ff.).*

- and what is implied about the atmosphere.

  Example: *The mass of people crowded into the tight space of the square implies an oppressive atmosphere (cf. lines 38 ff.).*

> **Language support: setting**
>
> The action takes place in …
> The setting is …
> The novel/scene is located in …
> The novel/scene is set in …
>
> This suggests/indicates/implies/gives the impression that …

The **language** an author uses helps to evoke the mood or atmosphere he wishes to create. The following aspects of language may be considered:

- **Allusions** or **connotations** of the words used. These may trigger positive or negative associations.

    Example: *Describing attendance as mandatory (cf. line 2) connotes the idea of forced and unwilling participation.*

- **Images** the author creates with his choice of language, e.g. comparisons made with metaphors or similes.

    Example: *The simile "Camera crews perched like buzzards" (line 13) suggests that every move is being watched and recorded. The comparison with buzzards – as birds of prey just waiting for the kill – creates a tense and dangerous atmosphere.*

- **Sentence structure**
    – Questions, explanations and commands can create a certain effect.

    Example: *"… who hasn't broken the law?" (line 31) This rhetorical question suggests that law-breaking is an everyday occurrence, however dangerous it might be, and stresses the restrictiveness of the society.*

    – The varying length of sentences can affect the atmosphere.

    Example: *"If not, you'll be imprisoned." (lines 4f.) This short sentence accentuates the fact that people have no choice but to obey. No long explanations or discussions are necessary.*

    – Word order or patterning may be used to create a certain effect on the reader. The repetition of certain words emphasizes their meaning. If parts of a sentence have the same structural pattern, this is known as parallelism.

    Example: *The repetition of the words, " … but carefully, carefully" (line 30) at the end of the sentence suggests that refusing to cooperate with the racketeers might be dangerous. This enhances the atmosphere of fear.*

b) Read the extract again and find more examples of the author's use of language and how this creates atmosphere.

B5 Taking into account the analysis of setting and atmosphere so far, consider how far the adjectives you chose in B3 are still appropriate. If necessary, reconsider your decision and find other examples from the extract.

7

A (brave) new world: What will the future bring?

B6 a) Read the next extract from the novel and say what event is described.

Extract 2 from "The Hunger Games" by Suzanne Collins

I find myself standing in a clump of sixteen-year-olds from the Seam. We exchange terse nods, then focus our attention on the temporary stage that is set up before the Justice Building. It
5 holds three chairs, a podium and two large glass balls, one for boys and one for girls. I stare at the paper slips in the girls' ball. Twenty-four of them have Katniss Everdeen written on them in careful handwriting.
10 Two of the three chairs fill with Madge's father, Mayor Undersee, who's a tall balding man, and Effie Trinket, District 12's escort, fresh from the Capitol with her scary white grin, pinkish hair and spring green suit. They murmur
15 to each other and look with concern at the empty seat.

Just as the town clock strikes two, the mayor steps up to the podium and begins to read. It's the same story every year. He tells the history of
20 Panem, the country that rose up out of the ashes of a place that was once called North America. He lists the disasters, the droughts, the storms, the fires, the encroaching[1] seas that swallowed up so much of the land, the brutal war for what
25 little sustenance[2] remained. The result was Panem, a shining capitol ringed by thirteen districts, which brought peace and prosperity to its citizens. Then came the Dark Days, the uprising of the Districts against the Capitol.
30 Twelve were defeated, the thirteenth obliterated. The Treaty of Treason gave us the new laws to guarantee peace and, as our yearly reminder that the Dark days must never be repeated, it gave us the Hunger Games.
35 The rules of the Hunger Games are simple. In punishment for the uprising, each of the twelve districts must provide one girl and one boy, called tributes, to participate. The twenty-four tributes will be imprisoned in a vast outdoor
40 arena that could hold anything from a burning desert to a frozen wasteland. Over a period of several weeks, the competitors must fight to the death. The last tribute standing wins.

Taking the kids from the districts, forcing
45 them to kill one another while we watch – this is the Capitol's way of reminding us how totally we are at their mercy. How little chance we would stand of surviving another rebellion. Whatever words they use, the real message is
50 clear. "Look how we take your children and sacrifice them and there's nothing you can do. If you lift a finger[3], we will destroy every last one of you. Just as we did in District Thirteen."

To make it humiliating as well as torturous,
55 the Capitol requires us to treat the Hunger Games as a festivity, a sporting event pitting every district against the others. The last tribute alive receives a life of ease back home, and their district will be showered with prizes, largely
60 consisting of food. All year, the Capitol will show the winning district gifts of grain and oil and even delicacies like sugar, while the rest of us battle starvation.

[…]
65 It's time for the drawing. Effie Trinket says as she always does, "Ladies first!" and crosses to the glass ball with the girls' names. She reaches in, digs her hand deep into the ball, and pulls out a slip of paper. The crowd draws in a collective
70 breath and then you can hear a pin drop[4], and I'm feeling nauseous and so desperately hoping that it's not me, that it's not me, that it's not me.

---

[1] **to encroach** = to cover more land gradually
[2] **sustenance** = food and drink
[3] **to lift a finger** = *here:* to show the first sign of revolt against the system
[4] **you can hear a pin drop** = this emphasizes how quiet a place is when no-one is talking

b) Read the extract again and collect further information about the vision of the future as revealed by the setting of the novel.

A (brave) new world: What will the future bring?

B7 Analyze how the setting and the language emphasize the atmosphere the author wishes to create.

> **Checklist**
> *Analyzing setting and language*
> ✓ Write a lead-in sentence which makes a general statement about the atmosphere evoked by the author. Example: *The choice of setting and language in the extract creates a … atmosphere.*
> ✓ Analyze the setting of the novel taking into account how it is described and what this implies about the atmosphere.
> ✓ Look closely at the language (connotations, imagery, sentence structure) and explain how it contributes to creating a particular atmosphere.
> ✓ Sum up your results in a concluding paragraph.

Language support	Language support: connotation
The image of … The metaphor/simile/symbol … … enhances … … describes … … depicts … … represents …	The word/phrase … alludes to … refers to … indicates … suggests … implies … connotes …

Language support	Language support: introductory sentence
The short/lengthy sentence … The sentence structure / word order / repetition … The use of parallelism … … underlines … … stresses … … accentuates … … emphasizes … … highlights …	The choice of setting and language in the extract creates a … atmosphere. The author's choice of setting and his use of language underline the general atmosphere of … Both the setting as well as the language used by the author … emphasize the … atmosphere of this scene.

Comment

B8 "Writers have always invented imaginary societies (utopias or dystopias) in order to comment on distinctive features and trends of their own societies" (Coral Ann Howells, 1995). Discuss whether this quotation can be applied to "The Hunger Games".

A (brave) new world: What will the future bring?

7

Getting to the point

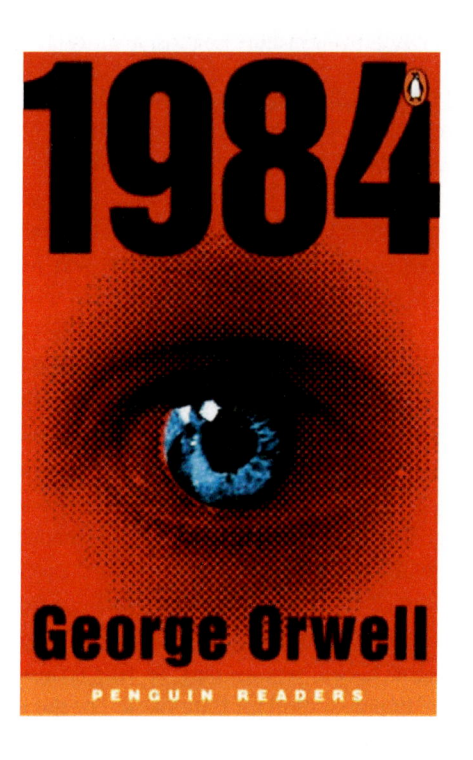

Pre-reading

C1 Think-pair-share: George Orwell's famous novel "1984" was written in 1949.

a) Note down what you know about society in the 1940s.

b) Speculate on how an author writing in that period might envision a dystopian future.

Comprehension

C2 Read the extract and summarize Orwell's vision of society in the novel "1984".

Checklist: Summary p. 124

Analysis

C3 Analyze the atmosphere created in this extract by examining the setting and the use of language.

Checklist: Text analysis p. 125

Comment

C4 Discuss whether Orwell's vision of the future as presented in this extract might still be relevant today. You might consider the following aspects:

- private and public surveillance and control
- propaganda and indoctrination
- economic and social deprivation.

Checklist: Comment pp. 126-127

Language support: comparison	
In comparison with/to …	Whereas …
In contrast to/with …	Conversely …
By comparison …	Likewise …/Similarly …

Language support: comparison and contrast	
Similarities	Differences
Orwell presents a foreboding vision of the future. Similarly, …/ Likewise, …/In a similar way, …/In a similar fashion, …	As opposed to …, Orwell's vision implies … Whereas today CCTV is under attack, the novel "1984" … Freedom of speech is an undisputed human right in democratic societies. Conversely, … In contrast to … By comparison, …

107

7 A (brave) new world: What will the future bring?

Extract from "1984" by George Orwell

It was a bright cold day in April, and the clocks were striking thirteen. Winston Smith, his chin nuzzled[1] into his breast in an effort to escape the vile wind, slipped quickly through the glass doors of Victory Mansions, though not quickly enough to prevent a swirl of gritty dust from entering along with him.

The hallway smelt of boiled cabbage and old rag mats. At one end of it a coloured poster, too large for indoor display, had been tacked to the wall. It depicted simply an enormous face, more than a metre wide: the face of a man of about forty-five, with a heavy black moustache and ruggedly handsome features. Winston made for the stairs. It was no use trying the lift. Even at the best of times it was seldom working, and at present the electric current was cut off during daylight hours. It was part of the economy drive[2] in preparation for Hate Week. The flat was seven flights up, and Winston, who was thirty-nine and had a varicose ulcer[3] above his right ankle, went slowly, resting several times on the way. On each landing, opposite the lift-shaft, the poster with the enormous face gazed from the wall. It was one of those pictures which are so contrived that the eyes follow you about when you move. BIG BROTHER IS WATCHING YOU, the caption beneath it ran.

Inside the flat a fruity voice was reading out a list of figures which had something to do with the production of pig-iron. The voice came from an oblong metal plaque like a dulled mirror which formed part of the surface of the right-hand wall. Winston turned a switch and the voice sank somewhat, though the words were still distinguishable. The instrument (the telescreen, it was called) could be dimmed[4], but there was no way of shutting it off completely. He moved over to the window: a smallish, frail figure, the meagreness of his body merely emphasized by the blue overalls which were the uniform of the party. His hair was very fair, his face naturally sanguine[5], his skin roughened by coarse soap and blunt razor blades and the cold of the winter that had just ended.

Outside, even through the shut window-pane, the world looked cold. Down in the street little eddies of wind were whirling dust and torn paper into spirals, and though the sun was shining and the sky a harsh blue, there seemed to be no colour in anything, except the posters that were plastered everywhere. The blackmoustachio'd face gazed down from every commanding corner. There was one on the house-front immediately opposite. BIG BROTHER IS WATCHING YOU, the caption said, while the dark eyes looked deep into Winston's own. Down at streetlevel another poster, torn at one corner, flapped fitfully[6] in the wind, alternately covering and uncovering the single word INGSOC. In the far distance a helicopter skimmed down between the roofs, hovered for an instant like a bluebottle, and darted away again with a curving flight. It was the police patrol, snooping into people's windows. The patrols did not matter, however. Only the Thought Police mattered.

Behind Winston's back the voice from the telescreen was still babbling away about pig-iron and the overfulfilment of the Ninth Three-Year Plan. The telescreen received and transmitted simultaneously. Any sound that Winston made, above the level of a very low whisper, would be picked up by it, moreover, so long as he remained within the field of vision which the metal plaque commanded, he could be seen as well as heard. There was of course no way of knowing whether you were being watched at any given moment. How often, or on what system, the Thought Police plugged in on any individual wire was guesswork. It was even conceivable that they watched everybody all the time. But at any rate they could plug in[7] your wire whenever they wanted to. You had to live – did live, from habit that became instinct – in the assumption that every sound you made was overheard, and, except in darkness, every movement scrutinized.

Winston kept his back turned to the telescreen. It was safer, though, as he well knew, even a back can be revealing. A kilometre away the Ministry of Truth, his place of work, towered vast and white above the grimy landscape. This, he thought with a sort of vague distaste[8] – this was London, chief city of Airstrip One, itself the third most populous of the provinces of Oceania. He tried to squeeze out some childhood memory

---

[1] **to nuzzle** = to press your nose / face against sth. gently
[2] **economy drive** = a big effort to save money
[3] **varicose ulcer** = a painful wound often found on the lower leg and caused by poor blood circulation
[4] **to be dimmed** = to turn down the volume and brightness of a device
[5] **sanguine** = confident and hopeful
[6] **fitfully** = starting and stopping often
[7] **to plug in** = here: to connect up with so.'s telescreen
[8] **distaste** = feeling of dislike

that should tell him whether London had always been quite like this. Were there always these vistas of rotting nineteenth-century houses, their sides shored up with baulks of timber[9], their windows patched with cardboard and their roofs with corrugated iron[10], their crazy garden walls sagging[11] in all directions? And the bombed sites where the plaster dust swirled in the air and the willow-herb straggled over the heaps of rubble; and the places where the bombs had cleared a larger patch and there had sprung up sordid colonies of wooden dwellings like chicken-houses? But it was no use, he could not remember: nothing remained of his childhood except a series of bright-lit tableaux occurring against no background and mostly unintelligible.

The Ministry of Truth – Minitrue, in Newspeak – was startlingly different from any other object in sight. It was an enormous pyramidal structure of glittering white concrete, soaring up, terrace after terrace, 300 metres into the air. From where Winston stood it was just possible to read, picked out on its white face in elegant lettering, the three slogans of the Party:

WAR IS PEACE

FREEDOM IS SLAVERY

IGNORANCE IS STRENGTH

The Ministry of Truth contained, it was said, three thousand rooms above ground level, and corresponding ramifications[12] below. Scattered about London there were just three other buildings of similar appearance and size. So completely did they dwarf[13] the surrounding architecture that from the roof of Victory Mansions you could see all four of them simultaneously. They were the homes of the four Ministries between which the entire apparatus of government was divided. The Ministry of Truth, which concerned itself with news, entertainment, education, and the fine arts. The Ministry of Peace, which concerned itself with war. The Ministry of Love, which maintained law and order. And the Ministry of Plenty, which was responsible for economic affairs. Their names, in Newspeak: Minitrue, Minipax, Miniluv, and Miniplenty.

The Ministry of Love was the really frightening one. There were no windows in it at all. Winston had never been inside the Ministry of Love, nor within half a kilometre of it. It was a place impossible to enter except on official business, and then only by penetrating through a maze of barbed-wire[14] entanglements[15], steel doors, and hidden machine-gun nests. Even the streets leading up to its outer barriers were roamed by gorilla-faced guards in black uniforms, armed with jointed truncheons[16].

---

[9] **baulk of timber** = *here*: a long, thick piece of wood
[10] **corrugated iron roof** = a roof made of iron shaped into parallel metal folds
[11] **sag** = to become soft and start to hang downwards
[12] **ramifications** = *here*: parts of sth. branching out from a main body
[13] **to dwarf sth.** = to make sth. seem small or unimportant
[14] **barbed-wire** = thick wire with a lot of sharp points on it
[15] **entanglement** = sth. which catches so. so they cannot get free easily
[16] **jointed truncheon** = a thick, bending stick which is carried as a weapon

8 Paying the price

Getting started

A1 a) Use the following questions to conduct a class survey:

How often do you shop for clothes?	every week / every month / every season
Do you follow the latest trends?	always / sometimes / never
How much do you spend every month?	less than €40 / €40-80 / more than €80
Where do you shop?	department stores / Internet / chains
Are fashion labels important for you?	absolutely / not really / not at all
How important are the clothes on a person you meet for the first time?	essential / not really important / irrelevant

b) Use the results of the survey to discuss how important fashion is for your class.

A2 a) Check the labels in your clothes and list the countries your clothes were produced in.

b) Point out what you find surprising, obvious, unexpected, predictable.

A3 a) Watch the trailer of the documentary "The true cost – the future is on sale" and describe the problems it highlights. www.diesterweg.de/cta/74014/links

b) Watch the trailer again and note down what pictures impressed you most. Give reasons.

c) Read the words in the box and match them with the definitions. Watch the trailer again if necessary.

> unprecedented – garment – sweatshop – unethical – working conditions – apparel – labour – developing countries – unsustainable

- A place where workers work hard for long hours at very low pay
- B synonyms for clothes (2)
- C not to be continued since it is not environmentally friendly
- D immoral/ignoring moral principles of dignity and respect/unwilling to accept rules of human conduct
- E never having happened before
- F synonym for work or work force
- G poor/having a low standard of living/having an ineffective economic system but trying to improve
- H referring to working hours, pay, safe working place

A4 In the film the expression "fast fashion" is used. You are already familiar with the term "fast food".
- Pair work: In two minutes note down the advantages and disadvantages of fast food.
- Compare your findings with another pair.
- Group work: Discuss to what extent the advantages and disadvantages of fast food can be applied to fast fashion.
- Find more advantages and disadvantages that specifically apply to fast fashion.

Skills
How to listen effectively
p. 152

Paying the price: Global fashion

8

A5 Group work (3)
  a) Choose one of the diagrams on pages 111 and 112 each, study it and present it to the other members of your group.
  b) Discuss what problems they reveal.

Diagram 1:

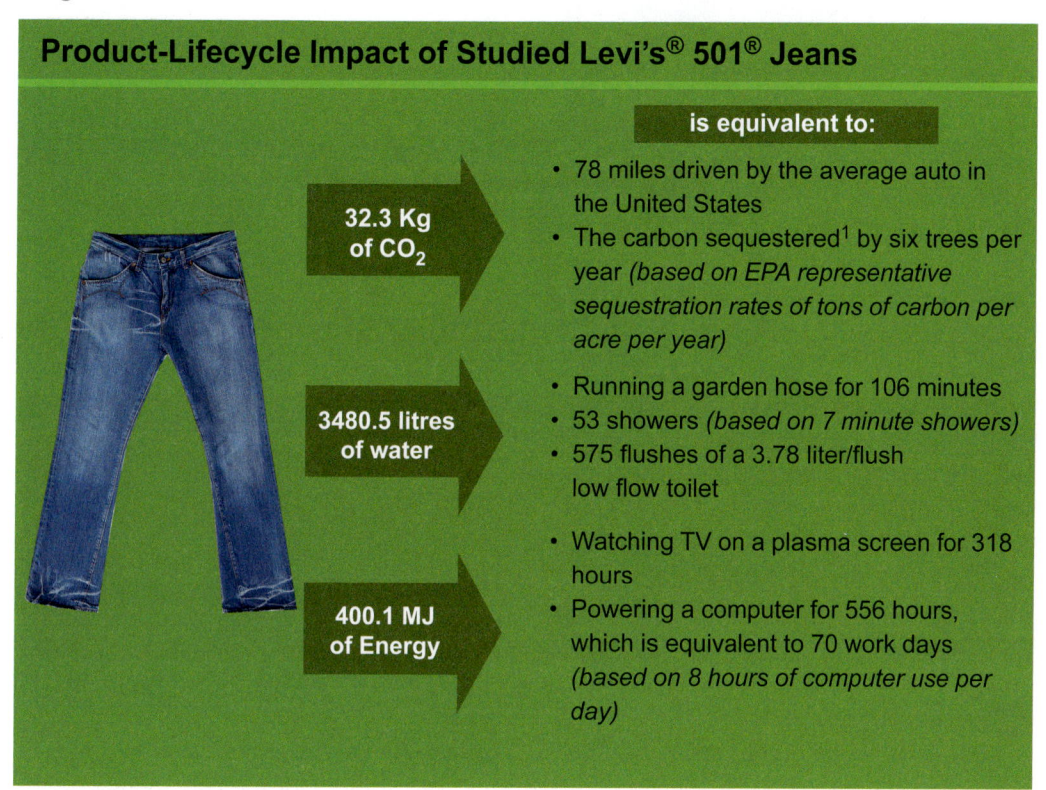

Product-Lifecycle Impact of Studied Levi's® 501® Jeans

is equivalent to:

32.3 Kg of CO_2
- 78 miles driven by the average auto in the United States
- The carbon sequestered[1] by six trees per year *(based on EPA representative sequestration rates of tons of carbon per acre per year)*

3480.5 litres of water
- Running a garden hose for 106 minutes
- 53 showers *(based on 7 minute showers)*
- 575 flushes of a 3.78 liter/flush low flow toilet

400.1 MJ of Energy
- Watching TV on a plasma screen for 318 hours
- Powering a computer for 556 hours, which is equivalent to 70 work days *(based on 8 hours of computer use per day)*

[1] **to sequester carbon** = when trees sequester carbon, they capture and store carbon dioxide (CO_2) from the atmosphere

Diagram 2:

HOW MUCH DOES IT COST TO MAKE A DENIM SHIRT IN BANGLADESH, VERSUS THE U.S.?

U.S — Total **$13.22**
- $0.75 Industrial laundry
- $5 Materials
- $7.47 Labour costs

Bangladesh — Total **$3.72**
- Industrial laundry $0.20
- Materials $3.30
- Labour costs $0.22

Paying the price: Global fashion

Diagram 3:

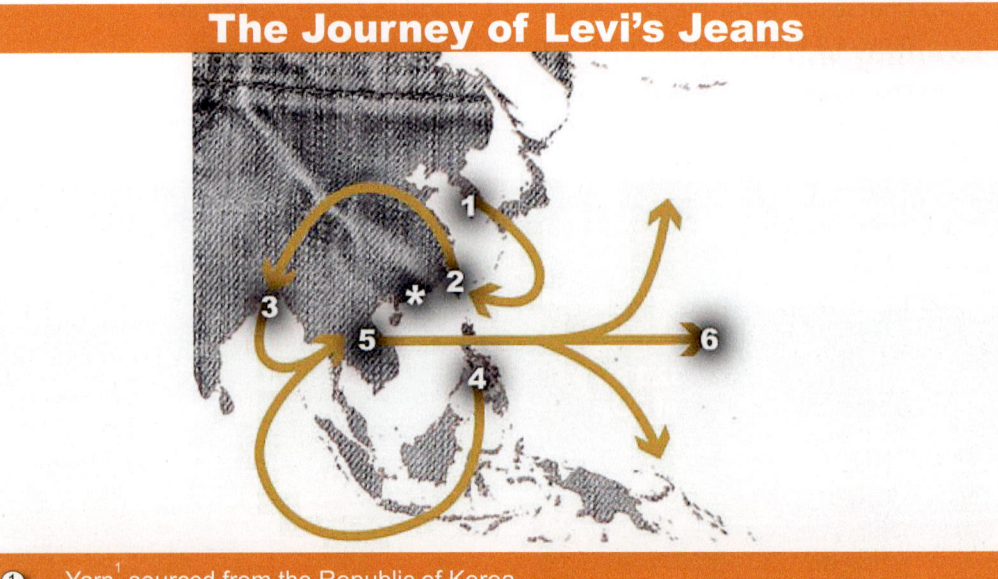

The Journey of Levi's Jeans

① Yarn¹ sourced from the Republic of Korea
② Fabric is woven and dyed in Taipei, China
③ Fabric is cut in Bangladesh
④ Zippers produced in the Philippines
⑤ Assembled into jeans in Cambodia
⑥ Exported to the rest of the world
✱ Li and Fung coordinates all activities from Hong Kong, China

¹ **yarn** = cotton, wool
graphic from http://www.aienetwork.org/

A6 Four corners:

a) Choose one of the statements from "The true cost – the future is on sale":

> "we are looking at a slave trade" (workers)

> "people have a preference to remain ignorant ... they will make an effort not to know" (consumers)

> "The big brands have been able to outsource their production ... They think they have outsourced responsibility" (production)

> "as we consume more we're using more resources and generating unprecedented amounts of waste" (environment)

b) Discuss it in your group.

c) Present your conclusion to the class.

Paying the price: Global fashion

Practice section

Listening and writing: Summary

In an exam, you may have to work on a task that combines listening and writing; for example first listen to a text on a certain topic and summarize it. Then you might be asked to read another text on the same topic, but often viewed from another angle, and analyze some aspects of that text. Finally, you can compare the two and draw your own conclusions on the topic at hand.

B1 a) Listening for gist: Watch the presentation by Helena Helmersson, Head of Corporate Responsibility, and Ann-Sofie Johansson, Head of Design at H&M once and note down keywords on the following aspects:

- subject
- main idea(s)
- purpose
- addressee(s)

www.diesterweg.de/cta/74014/links

How to listen effectively p. 152

b) Read the following statements (1-4) and use your notes to decide which one best sums up the gist of the presentation:

The presentation by Helena Helmersson, Head of Corporate Responsibility, and Ann-Sofie Johansson, Head of Design at H&M deals with ...

1) ... H&M's efforts to use more sustainable materials like hemp in their clothes.

2) ... celebrities that wear H&M's sustainable fashion on the red carpet.

3) ... H&M's efforts to make fashion that is attractive as well as produced sustainably.

4) ... H&M's programmes aimed at educating and controlling their suppliers and helping their families.

Paying the price: Global fashion

B2 a) Now listen again and list as many words and phrases as possible for the following categories:

materials	fashion/clothes	production cycle	addressing challenges
recycled polyester	fashion brands	suppliers	sustainability report
hemp	...	to increase one's profit	code of conduct
...		...	...

b) Look up any words you do not know.

B3 a) Listening for detail: Listen again and answer the following questions in a few words. Where possible, use the vocabulary you collected in B2a).

- What are H&M's main goals when making their products? Name two aspects.
- How do they want to ensure that the conditions in their suppliers' factories are acceptable? Name two measures.
- What role does the environment play in their business?
- What is special about their new collection? Name three aspects.
- How does H&M try to improve the lives of the people living where the cotton for their products is grown and harvested? Name three measures.
- How do they describe their customers? Name two adjectives.

b) Summarize how H&M wants to enable their customers to

"enjoy fashion without feeling guilty".

Use your notes from B3a).
Begin your summary with the introductory sentence from B1b).

Skills
How to listen effectively
p. 152

Skills
Checklist: Summary
p. 124

Paying the price: Global fashion

Reading and writing: Analysis

B4 a) Pre-reading: Based on what you have already learned about "fast fashion", think of possible controversial aspects of H&M's business model and list them. Talk about your ideas with a partner and compare your lists.

b) Reading: Read the excerpt from Maddy Newman's blog. Add any new points to your list.

c) In your lists, highlight controversial aspects raised by Newman (whether shared by you or not). Use these points to state Newman's message and name the aim of her blog.

H&M's megastore in Melbourne houses over one million items of fashion, accessories and homewares.

Why I'm Not Excited About H&M's Australian Launch

by Maddie Newman 7/4/14

As H&M opened the doors to its first Australian store in Melbourne over the weekend, fashion media and consumers alike were chomping at the bit[1] for the retailer's dirt-cheap 'fast fashion'.
5 Labelled by some as "the best thing to happen in Australia all year", H&M's 5000-square metre, three-level megastore in Melbourne's GPO building houses[2] over one million items of fashion, accessories and homewares[3], and all at
10 prices so cheap that you needn't think twice before buying.

And therein lies the problem. Well, one of the problems. H&M, with their $6.95 tanks[4] and $12.95 jeans, encourage the kind of mindless
15 consumerism that fast fashion thrives off — buy cheap and buy lots. The proliferation of wallet-

[1] **to chomp at the bit** = to be anxious and ready to do sth.
[2] **to house** = to be a place where sth. is kept
[3] **homeware** = crockery and furniture which are used to furnish a house or room
[4] **tank** = tank-top

115

friendly clothes and accessories that are 'designer-inspired' (a lovely little euphemism for 'shameless rip-off'[5]) has led many to confuse this increasing disposability of fashion with 'democratisation'.

But with cheap prices, the victor isn't really the consumer — it's the fast fashion empires. Quantity over quality is a horribly unsustainable approach, but it's the reason why H&M Chairman Stefan Persson is making mad bank[6] (est. $32.8 billion), and also why most of our fast fashion purchases literally fall apart at the seams before even coming close to the 30th wear (the number recommended by sustainability journalist, Lucy Siegle).

Fast Fashion's Hidden Costs

Fast fashion's seductively low prices encourage us to buy things we don't need (and sometimes don't really want) with little regard for the enormous environmental and human costs of this rapid-fire supply chain that squeezes margin from those who are most vulnerable — garment workers in developing nations halfway across the world. H&M are estimated to produce 20-25% of their products in Bangladesh, making them the largest player in the country, and while they have gone some way to working towards a living wage (they aim to pay their workers a living wage by 2018), Labour Behind The Label — a UK-based collective of trade unions, charities and consumer organisations who work to support workers' rights — argues that H&M's projects "do not show evidence of delivering a living wage for workers any time soon" and that they have yet to put a figure on what the living wage actually is. H&M don't own any of their own factories, and while they require their direct suppliers to sign a Code of Conduct and are subject to their Full Audit Program[7], they acknowledge that they don't have direct contact with or influence over "second-tier" suppliers[8]. It's this lack of transparency in supply chains that leads to exploitation of workers, and in extreme cases, tragedies like Rana Plaza last April.

To be fair, though, as far as fast fashion empires go, H&M is not all evil. In fact, it was recently named as one of the 'World's Most Ethical Companies' according to Ethisphere for its leadership in signing the Bangladeshi Accord on Fire and Building Safety, as well as its 'Conscious Exclusive' collection made from sustainable materials. It is also one of the world's largest buyers of organic cotton. But these achievements are dwarfed[9] by the sheer amount of resources used to make the estimated 550 million garments it sells each year.

Fast fashion is a huge drain on the environment — the textile industry is one of world's largest users and polluters of water, thanks to the prevalence[10] of cotton (a very thirsty plant grown in mostly dry regions like India, Mali and southern USA), as well as the many chemicals and dyes used in treating fabric. A single pair of jeans uses up to 5678 litres of water, and emits the same amount of carbon dioxide as driving 125 km. No matter how many 'conscious collections' H&M produce, as long as they make more and more clothes, their impact on the environment is significant. As Siegle wrote in her analysis of H&M's 2012 sustainability report, "Despite an understanding of all the pressures on Planet Earth sketched out in the report, there are no plans to scale back on ambition or indeed inventory."

[...]

There's no doubt the retailer, like Topshop and Zara before it, will find massive success in the Australian market — we do love a bargain. But if you find yourself in line this week at the Melbourne store, among the thousands of other shoppers, please take a moment to think about the true cost of your $12.95 skinny jeans.

---

[5] **rip-off** = *(slang)* sth. that is more expensive than it should be
[6] **bank** = *here:* profit
[7] **audit program** = a set of policies and procedures that determine how a business is evaluated
[8] **"second-tier" suppliers** = a company that supplies materials or parts to another company that then supplies them to a manufacturer
[9] **to be dwarfed by sth.** = to be made to look smaller or less important by sth.
[10] **prevalence** = the fact that sth. is very common in a place

Paying the price: Global fashion

B5 Newman uses a specific kind of language to persuade her readers that the "hidden costs" of cheap fashion might be too high. To understand her persuasive strategies it is helpful to examine the choice of words and the imagery she uses.

a) Read the two info-boxes:

Info: Choice of words

An author uses specific words in order to serve a certain purpose. Examples of such purposes are: to create a special mood or to be particularly persuasive. The following aspects may be considered:

- **the literal meaning of a word**
  Example: Newman talks about the "disposability" (l. 20) of clothes, underlining how fast the business has become and how short-lived its products are.

- **the connotative meaning of a word** (i.e. what feelings it evokes, what you associate with it)
  Example: Fashion like the one produced by H&M is referred to as "dirt-cheap" (l. 4). The use of the word "dirt" here emphasizes Newman's critical attitude towards this kind of fashion and particularly its low prices, because "dirt" is something foul and nasty. It becomes evident that the cheap rates are an unhealthy development which reduces the value of the work needed

- **the word field** (i.e the specific subject a word/set of words belongs to)
  Example: Describing the production cycle of fast fashion as a "rapid-fire supply chain" (l. 34) is another example of how negatively this industry is portrayed by Newman. Rapid-fire is a term from the semantic field of war and likens fast fashion to a military strategy that is not only fast, but also cruel and potentially lethal.

Info: Imagery

"Imagery" refers to the use of images an author creates in the reader's mind in order to underline his/her message.
The following types of images are often found in persuasive texts:

- **simile** (a comparison of two ideas, often linked by "as" or "like")
  Example: "'designer-inspired' […] for 'shameless rip-off'" (ll. 17-19)

- **metaphor** (two ideas that are normally not linked are compared in a metaphor without using "as" or "like")
  Example: "rapid-fire supply chains" (l. 34)

- **personification** (attribution of human traits to things or concepts)
  Example: "mad bank" (l. 25)

---

b) Look at the examples of the author's choice of words and imagery in the grid on page 118. Complete the grid.

c) Add three more quotations to the grid.

d) Pair work: Swap grids with a partner. Suggest interpretations and functions for your partner's new examples. Then talk about your results.

Paying the price: Global fashion

example/quotation	effect	function
"dirt-cheap" (l. 4)	"cheap", in itself a word that can have positive as well as negative connotations, is made to sound (more?) negative by adding "dirt" to it	first clue that "cheap" may not always be "good"
"wallet-friendly clothes" (ll. 16-17)		
"fast fashion empires" (l. 22)		describes both the size of the companies and their business style
"Stefan Persson is making mad bank (est. $ 32.8 billion)" (ll. 24-25)		
"rapid-fire supply chain" (l. 34)	"supply chain" is put into an almost militaristic context and gets a negative connotation	
"squeeze[s] margin" (l. 34)		

e) Analyze how Newman uses special words and phrases as well as images to persuade her readers that the "true cost" (l. 96) of cheap fashion might be too high.

> **Checklist**
> ✓ Collect words and phrases the author chose to make her point.
> ✓ Use the literal meaning, connotative meaning or semantic field to analyze and explain the words' significance or function.
> ✓ Examine how the author uses imagery to underline her message.
> ✓ Do not analyze words and phrases in an isolated, additive way.
> ✓ Analyze and explain the words and phrases in their context within the text.
> ✓ Refer back to the task and your overall claim.

Comment

B6 Naturally, the PR presentation by H&M shows the company's efforts in a very positive light. Maddy Newman presents a different view in her blog.

Write a convincing, well-structured comment for Newman's website where you present your view on H&M's efforts. Explain whether you agree with her when she claims that H&M's Australian launch is nothing to be excited about, but rather gives reason to worry about the phenomenon called "fast fashion".

Follow these steps:

1. Review your notes on the presentation by H&M and Newman's arguments. Highlight arguments that you find particularly convincing.
2. Determine your own view on the problem.
3. Find more arguments to support your view.
4. Collect examples and illustrations to make your arguments more persuasive.
5. Use the fashion phrases you collected in A3c) and B2a).
6. Structure your comment according to the requirements.
7. Use appropriate vocabulary.

Paying the price: Global fashion

Getting to the point

Pre-listening

C1 Complete these sentences:

The responsible consumer ...
  ... is aware of ...
  ... does not ...
  ... is considerate of ...
  ... buys ...
  ... wears ...
  ... tries to ...

C2 Match the following words and expressions (1-11) with the definitions (A-K). You will need them to understand the podcast.

> 1. thrift store – 2. chain – 3. bargain shopping – 4. turnover – 5. shipment – 6. merchandise – 7. mark-up – 8. high-end designers – 9. low-wage countries – 10. resources – 11. manufacturing centres

A (natural) supplies of sth. that a country has and can use, e.g. minerals, oil
B a group of shops owned by the same company
C the total amount of goods sold by a company during a particular period of time
D the process of sending goods from one place to another
E an increase in the price of sth. based on the difference between the cost of producing it and the price it is sold at
F goods that are for sale in a store
G designers that produce expensive clothes of high quality
H looking for and buying goods sold at prices that are lower than usual
I shop that sells used goods; often the profits go to charity
J (often developing) countries where workers are paid very low wages and therefore production costs are low
K places/countries with a lot of companies that produce goods

Comprehension

C3 Listen to the podcast and point out how Elizabeth Cline used to shop, how that has changed and what consequences for her as well as for others are dealt with in the podcast.

www.diesterweg.de/cta/74014/links

Skills
How to listen effectively
p. 152

Analysis

C4 Read the blog entry on "upcycling" on page 120 and analyze how Chris Long uses arguments and a certain kind of language to convince his readers that upcycling is worth a try.

Upcycling industry takes a bite[1] out of national waste stream[2]

by Chris Long on December 16, 2013

"I got the idea on Pinterest" is a phrase that's been cropping up more and more often in mainstream conversation. Whereas uniquely repurposed[3] milk bottles and aprons-made-from-old-curtains used to be limited to the realm of dedicated crafters and Martha Stewart fanatics, upcycling — the art of creating something new from otherwise discarded materials — is reaching a far broader range of society. And it's a wonderful thing.

Not only is upcycling encouraging more people to look at what they have in a new light, it's also making people think twice before tossing something in the trash. And this don't-buy-it-if-you-can-make-it mentality is already having a positive impact on our environment and, more particularly, on our landfills[4].

Let's face it, while most of us understand that the needs of modern cultures far outpace the resources available to us, the majority of us don't consider the problem when we're, say, buying a cheap new outfit or tossing out last year's jeans. In fact, most Americans throw away 70 pounds of clothing and textiles every year, while the textile industry generates more than 13 million tons a year, or 5.2 percent of the total municipal solid waste generation.

But by promoting the practice of upcycling, we're starting to take a bite out of that number. In 2006, for example, 2.5 billion pounds of fabric were kept from the landfills by used-clothing purchases. By 2011, fabric recycling was up to 3.2 billion pounds.

[…]

Even if you're not recycling or upcycling every item or even one in several items that come through your house, taking a moment to consider what could be done with an object before tossing it out can make a difference. Instead of tossing out an old sweater, for example, consider using the material to make socks or a bag. Repaint old mugs with bake-on ceramic paint or use old bath faucets as towel hooks. The ideas are endless and idea-generating sites are encouraging more and more users to jump on the upcycling wagon:

Pinterest: With five million articles pinned per day and climbing, Pinterest is one of the top sites for sparking[5] your upcycling imagination.

Etsy: An online community of one-person and small business operations, Etsy provides plenty of upcycling inspiration through shared images, sale items and blogs.

Instructables: Having a hard time figuring out how to pull off an upcycling project? Check out the Instructables website for helpful hints and step-by-step guides.

As upcycling and zero waste move more into the mainstream, we need to do what we can to encourage the process and drive others to look at everyday items in a new light. And the best way to get there is to lead by example.

---

[1] **to take a bite out of sth.** = to reduce sth.
[2] **waste stream** = complete flow of waste from domestic or industrial areas to final disposal
[3] **to repurpose sth.** = to change sth. so that it can be used for a different purpose
[4] **landfill** = a large hole in the ground where waste is buried
[5] **to spark sth.** = to make sth. happen

Comment

C5 Compare the approach towards clothes/fashion/shopping from the podcast with the one advocated in the blog. Comment on the question whether "upcycling" really is an alternative to so-called "fast fashion".

Mediation

In a global world mediation becomes a more and more important technique as people from different countries might need to be informed about a topic that is presented in a language they do not understand. They need someone to explain the content of the text to them. This means that in mediation you should not translate a text word by word but try to convey the most important points.

To work on mediation tasks successfully you need to keep the following in mind:
- purpose
- text type
- addressee

D1 You are an intern at H&M in London. On the net you have found this article about the opening of a Primark store in Germany. As your employers are interested in the expansion of Primark into the German market, they ask you to summarize the main information in a report for them.

> **Mediation task**
>
> *Write a report for the company in which you summarize the most important facts about the opening of the Primark store in Cologne. Include information on the new shop itself, its importance for the Primark strategy in Germany, the motivation and reaction of consumers.*

In order to do this, follow these steps:

a) Skim the article and find out what it is about.

b) Before you read the article a second time, determine what type of text is expected for your mediation.

c) Read the article carefully, find relevant passages and note down key words and/or key sentences in English.

d) Write your report in English. Remember to stick to the facts and to use a formal register.

Tausende bei Primark-Eröffnung

Erstellt 02.05.2014

Großer Ansturm zur Eröffnung der ersten Primark-Filiale in Köln. Bereits in den frühen Morgenstunden warteten tausende Menschen vor der Neumarkt-Galerie und harrten stundenlang aus. Einer der wichtigsten Gründe: Der Preis. *Von Corinna Schulz*

Innenstadt

Die ersten hatten sich schon um sechs Uhr morgens an den Absperrgittern vor der Neumarkt Galerie eingefunden. Kurz vor der Eröffnung der ersten Kölner Filiale des irischen Textil-Giganten Primark um zehn Uhr reichte die Schlange der jungen, meist weiblichen Shopping-Willigen schon durch die gesamte Zeppelinstraße bis zum Neumarkt. Ihr Ziel: Schnellstmöglich an die Regale, wo sich T-Shirts, Jeans, Blusen und Röcke stapeln und die leeren Einkaufstaschen, die schon vor der Tür verteilt wurden, füllen.

Auf vier Etagen und mehr als 8000 Quadratmetern bietet Primark 5000 Modeartikeln für Frauen, Männer und Kinder. Knapp 800 Mitarbeiter beschäftigt das Unternehmen in Köln, davon 100 in Vollzeit. Es ist der zwölfte Laden der Kette in Deutschland.

„Mit unserem Store haben wir hier in Köln ein so großes Angebot wie kaum sonst in Deutschland", sagte Primark-Chefin Breege O'Donoghue während der Eröffnungsfeier zu der neben Wirtschaftsdezernentin Ute Berg auch der irische Botschafter Michael Collins kam. Und die Managerin verriet: „Mein komplettes Outfit heute kostet 42 Euro plus 10 Euro, für das, was man nicht sieht."

Der Preis ist auch für Lena (16) einer der wichtigsten Gründe, warum sich die Kölner Schülerin zwei Stunden in die Warteschlange gestellt hat. „Für ein T-Shirt zahle ich 2,50 Euro, eine Jeans gibt es für acht Euro. Da bekomme ich für mein Taschengeld schon eine riesen Tüte und die Klamotten sind echt hipp". Zusammen mit ihrer Freundin Carlotta (15), die in der Schule keinen Brückentag hat, sondern schwänzt, wird im sogenannten Showroom ausgiebig probiert. Neben über 80 Umkleidekabinen hat Primark auch einen großen Raum eingerichtet, wo die Kunden vor den Wandspiegeln gegenseitig ihre Outfits begutachten können. Ideal für die zwei Freundinnen. Ein schwarzer Minirock für vier Euro wandert nach kurzem Schaulaufen ebenso in Lenas Einkaufskorb wie zwei Paar Sandalen und mehrere Oberteile. An der Kasse zahlt die 16-jährige nur knapp 30 Euro für ein komplett neues Outfit.

Paying the price: Global fashion

> **Checklist**
> *Mediation*
>
> **Dos**
> - Focus on all the essential aspects that are necessary to provide the information required.
> - Leave out unimportant details that are not relevant for the addressee but make sure the wh-questions are answered (here: the company you are working for).
> - If necessary explain facts and terms the addressee might not be familiar with.
> - Leave out personal statements or comments.
> - Use a style that corresponds to the required text type and the addressee. As you have to write a report for a company, make sure you use a factual presentation, a neutral choice of words and a formal register.
>
> **Don'ts**
> - Do not translate literally.
> - Do not follow the structure of the original text but feel free to reorganize the information according to your purpose (here: providing information on marketing strategies and consumer reaction).
> - Do not add information which is not given in the text.
> - Do not use direct speech but transfer it into reported speech where necessary, using verbs like say, claim, believe, suggest, etc.

D2 Peer-editing:

a) Exchange your text with a partner. Read it carefully and correct any language mistakes.

b) Use the checklist on mediation to see if the text fulfills all the requirements. Give special consideration to the choice of information and to the wording.

c) Make suggestions to improve the text where necessary.

d) Use your partner's feedback to correct your text.

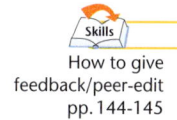

Skills
How to give feedback/peer-edit
pp. 144-145

Checklist: Summary

A summary is for someone who has not read the text and needs to know the essence of what it is about. The readers of your summary do not expect you to go into detail; instead they want a short version of the text. Therefore, a written summary only gives a general idea of what the text is about and the most important information.

Dos	**Before writing:**
	✓ Read the text carefully and highlight key words and/or key sentences.
	✓ Divide the text up into parts or sub-sections.
	✓ Find an appropriate sentence or keywords to summarize each sub-section.
	Writing an introduction:
	✓ The introductory sentence of your summary should include the author, title, type of text, the place and date of publication, and the main idea. In other words, you need to answer these wh-questions:
	  ✓ **Who** is the author?
	  ✓ **When** was the text published?
	  ✓ **Where** was it published?
	  ✓ **What** type of text is it?
	  ✓ **What** topic does the text deal with? State the underlying problem or conflict, and not simply its content.
	Writing the main part:
	✓ The main part of your summary connects the highlighted passages and the summaries or key words of the sub-sections.
	✓ Focus on the essentials/on basic facts.
	✓ Use the present tense.
	✓ Use your own words.
	✓ Use formal language.
	✓ Use connectives to link your sentences.

Don'ts	✓ Don't include irrelevant details. ✓ Don't use the present progressive. ✓ Don't use quotations or direct speech. ✓ Don't give your personal opinion. ✓ Don't start analyzing the text. ✓ Don't try to create suspense.
Language support	**Introduction:** ✓ *The short story/novel/article/poem … "[title]" …* ✓ *The extract from the … "[title]" … by [author] …* ✓ *… written by [author] in [year] …* ✓ *… written by [author] and published in [year/source]…* ✓ *… deals with/is about/shows/illustrates …* **Stating the topic/purpose of a text:** ✓ *The text/story … is about/shows/presents/depicts/alludes to/refers to/ criticizes/targets/comments on/exposes … the fact that/the problem of …* ✓ See page 141 for more language support to connect your sentences. **Main part:** ✓ *According to the author, …* ✓ *The author believes/claims/emphasizes/states/points out …* ✓ *From the author's point of view, …* ✓ *The author is of the opinion that …*

Checklist: Text analysis

When writing a text analysis, analyzing chronologically often seems easier, but can be problematic if your task is to concentrate on a certain aspect of the text you are analyzing. Plan your text well before you start writing your analysis to find out whether a chronological or an aspect-oriented analysis works better. If you are supposed to analyze a development, for example, a chronological analysis might work better. If you are examining a certain character, you should concentrate on relevant aspects.

Always examine the (stylistic/rhetorical/structural/ …) devices the author uses and explain why they are used/what they support and what their effect on the reader is. Like in any other text, your text should follow the structure of **introduction – main part – conclusion** (see pp. 138-139).

Dos	✓ Begin with a central claim. In order to do that, keep the central message or problem of the text in mind, but also the task you are working on. ✓ Structure your text logically; analyze the text either chronologically or aspect-oriented. ✓ Distinguish between types of texts. When you analyze prose, for example, narrative techniques are especially important. When you analyze poetry, pay special attention to rhyme and rhythm. And when you analyze non-fictional texts, the argumentative structure may be the most relevant aspect. ✓ Give examples for important stylistic devices (direct or indirect quotations), explain them/their meaning and analyze their effect on the reader. ✓ Always combine findings on language/structure and content/message. ✓ Use the present tense. ✓ Use connectives to link your ideas. Look at page 141 for help. ✓ Use formal and neutral language. ✓ End with a conclusion that doesn't only sum up your findings, but also refers back to the task and states your results on a more abstract level.
Don'ts	✓ Don't use the past tense. ✓ Don't only paraphrase the text you are analyzing. ✓ Don't speculate – you must use evidence from the text to support your findings. ✓ Don't write about every detail.
Language support	**Writing about language/style:** ✓ *formal/informal/colloquial/vulgar/academic/clear/objective/vivid/… language* ✓ *complex/simple sentences* ✓ *a serious/friendly/humorous/ironic/polite/rude/critical/optimistic/… tone* ✓ *The style of the text is plain/condensed/vivid/pompous/artificial/…* **Writing about stylistic/rhetorical devices:** ✓ *The author uses metaphorical language to …* ✓ *The author employs stylistic devices to …* ✓ *The author uses figures of speech to …* ✓ *The stylistic devices underline/enhance the arguments/message of the text.* ✓ *The stylistic device supports/affirms the author's/the text's message.* ✓ *The stylistic device/metaphor/… brings out the message …* ✓ *to describe/depict …* ✓ *to examine/explain/analyze the stylistic devices* ✓ *to make a comparison …* **Writing about characters, atmosphere, situations:** ✓ *to make use of/use … to create a … atmosphere*

Checklist: Comment

In a comment you are asked to give your opinion and explain it. This could be in response to something that has happened or on the views expressed in a newspaper article, discussion etc. When commenting on an issue, you should not only pay attention to arguments and the correct use of language (grammar, choice of words, etc.), but also to the structure of your text. Like in any other text, your text should follow the structure of **introduction – main part – conclusion** (see pp. 139-140).

Before you start writing, it is necessary to think about how you can present your ideas most effectively in a sequence of paragraphs. Moreover, you should make the relationship between your points clear by using connectives, e.g. to point out contrasts and contradictions.

Dos	**Plan the structure of your comment to include the following parts.** **Introduction:** ✓ Try to get your reader's attention by starting in an interesting way. ✓ Include the topic/question you will write about as outlined in the task. **Main part:** ✓ Identify and refer to the arguments put forward in the text. ✓ Clearly state your own opinion on the topic. ✓ Weigh up and reply to arguments that do not support your point of view. ✓ Include evidence to support/refute arguments (expert opinions; statistics etc.). ✓ Base your arguments on facts and put them forward coherently and unemotionally – that is more convincing. **Conclusion:** ✓ Sum up your arguments. ✓ Come to a logical conclusion about the topic/question stating your opinion. **Organize your ideas coherently:** ✓ Organize your ideas into paragraphs. ✓ Link your ideas/paragraphs with connectives. Look at page 141 for help. **Use formal language:** ✓ Use connectives (*in addition, finally, moreover, however,* etc.). ✓ Use the passive voice occasionally. ✓ Try to avoid using "I" too frequently. There are many other ways of expressing your opinion.
Don'ts	✓ Don't start writing before you have planned your answer and know what conclusion you will come to. ✓ Don't just state arguments/opinions without supporting them. ✓ Don't use informal language, e.g. short forms (*don't, can't*, etc.), colloquial language (*kids, gonna*, etc.) or slang.

Checklist: Comment

Language support

Introduction:
Referring to the topic/question:
- This comment/answer will discuss/consider/argue …
- The problem/issue to be discussed in this comment is …
- The text/article/story/author … raises the question of/introduces the problem of …, which will be discussed in this comment.
- … is a topic that has given rise to serious discussions over …
- … is a hotly-debated topic right now as …
- … seems important to weigh up the benefits and drawbacks of …

Main part:
Identifying and referring to arguments:
- The main problem/issue/question that is touched upon in this article is …
- The author states/argues/claims/maintains/supports the idea/puts forward the argument/denies the fact/contradicts the opinion that …

Presenting your own opinion:
- It is my belief/opinion that …/In my opinion …/Personally …
- As far as I can see/am concerned …/As I see it …
- I (completely) agree/(absolutely) disagree with …
- As opposed to … I (strongly) believe that …

Weighing up and countering arguments:
- Taking into account what has been said so far, I …
- Having considered the different arguments, I …/Considering the fact that …
- On the one hand …, on the other hand …
- Whereas girls generally like to use the Internet to …, boys prefer to use it to …
- In contrast to A, B …
- Looking at the problem from A's side, you have to admit that …
- Another important point/factor/argument to consider is …
- Supporters/Opponents of … argue/might argue that …
- Others claim/assert that …
- While there is no doubt/question that …, … must also be considered/mentioned.
- It must also be taken into consideration that …

Conclusion:
- All in all, it can be said that …
- In conclusion, I would like to say that …
- After weighing up the arguments carefully, I come to the conclusion that …
- Having looked at the issue from different points of view, I firmly believe that …
- To conclude, …
- To sum up, …

Checklist: Creative writing

A. Continuation of a prose text

You may be asked to continue a prose text you have read or write a passage from the point of view of one of the characters in the story. You need to write in a similar way as the author. Pay attention to the author's style and the developments in the story. Decide if your development is plausible and fits in with what has happened before.

Dos	

	Content:
	✓ Stay in line with the plot and atmosphere.
	✓ You are not entirely free as you are expected to show in your text production that you have digested the original text. So you have to use the information from that text as a basis for a plausible sequel.
	✓ Mention certain features (places, details of landscape or weather) that have been introduced.
	✓ Make sure you present the characters in a way that does not contradict their previous behaviour unless this change in character is part of your story.
	✓ If possible refer back to events in the text you have dealt with.
	
	Point of view (narrative perspective):
	✓ Adopt the same narrative perspective:
	  • First person narrator
	  • Third person narrator
	    • Omniscient (knowing and commenting on all the characters' thoughts and feelings, foreshadowing future events) or
	    • Limited (having an insight into one of the character's thoughts and feelings only).
	
	Language:
	✓ Stay in line with the author's style and try to imitate it.
	✓ Consider the amount of narrative, descriptive as opposed to dramatic passages that mainly consist of dialogue.
	✓ Use either long, elaborate sentences or short simple ones like the author.
	✓ Employ imagery (symbolic or metaphorical language) if it occurs in the original text; you need not always think of new images but pick up the ones used and extend them.
	✓ Adopt the author's use of language to place a character in a particular social class or reveal his/her emotions.

Checklist: Creative writing

B. Change of perspective

You may be asked to consider the fictional situation from the point of view of a different character. This can be done in
- a dialogue
- a diary entry/an interior monologue
- a letter to a friend.

Dos	**Content:** ✓ Consider the relationship between the characters involved, their age, their social standing, the way they might be personally affected by what has happened. ✓ Imagine how they would feel in the circumstances. ✓ Decide how you would comment on other characters and their behaviour. **Language:** ✓ Age, relationship, social class and profession determine the way a person speaks. ✓ Make sure you use an appropriate register (formal, informal, colloquial, scientific, educated). ✓ Emotions may alter a person's behaviour and speech. ✓ Use typical elements of spoken language like exclamations, incomplete sentences (ellipses), questions, etc.
Don'ts	✓ Don't stray from the original text you were given. ✓ Don't create an entirely new universe. ✓ Don't write in your personal style, but adopt the style of the author. ✓ Don't quote when you refer back to instances in the original text. Make the references part of your own narrative.
Language support	✓ In a prose text you can reveal the speaker's feelings not only in his/her words but also in his/her body language, you could even contrast the two levels. ✓ The following verbs can help you: *admit, agree, whisper, shout, cry, scream, deny, accept, convince, persuade, shrug, stammer, nod, wince, declare, laugh, smile, grin, smirk, confide, concede, frown, mutter, mumble, insult, accuse, wink,* etc.

Checklist: Formal letter

There are many different types of formal letters that you could be expected to write, e.g. a letter of request, a letter of inquiry, a letter of complaint, a letter of application, often called a covering letter. Whatever the kind of letter it is, the response you get will greatly depend on the way the letter is written. Formal letters are generally precise and to the point, without unnecessary detail.

It is also important that you adopt the right tone i.e. it should sound business-like rather than emotional. Finally you must also think about the layout of your letter and the type of language you use. The language used in this type of letter should not be chatty and personal but rather formal and reserved.

Before you start writing you should first ask yourself:
- Who am I writing to?
- What do I need to tell them?
- Why am I writing?
- What do I want them to do?

Dos	**Before writing:**
	✓ Observe the rules for the layout of a formal letter (see below).
	✓ Use formal language.
	✓ Choose a more formal font for your letter or email if you use a computer, e.g. Times New Roman or Arial
	✓ Draft and edit your letter or email before you send it. Poor grammar and punctuation or spelling mistakes do not make a good impression.
	✓ Plan the structure of your letter to include the following parts:
	Salutation and introduction:
	✓ Address the person you are writing to correctly:
	• If you know the person's name write: *Dear Ms* (for a woman whose marital status is not known) *Mrs, Mr, Dr Smith,* etc.
	• If you do not know the person's name: *Dear Sir or Madam,*
	✓ Start the first sentence with a capital letter.
	✓ State the purpose of your letter in the first paragraph.
	✓ Refer to any correspondence that may already have taken place.
	Main part:
	✓ Organize your ideas in paragraphs.
	✓ Include important and/or relevant details such as exact names, dates and addresses, e.g. where you saw the job advertised, when and where you bought the defective goods etc.
	✓ Keep to the point and avoid unnecessary details.
	✓ Be polite and tactful.
	Conclusion and ending:
	✓ Outline how you expect the recipient to react, e.g. send you information, give you a refund, reply to your application etc.
	✓ End the letter in the appropriate way:
	• *Yours sincerely* if you address them by name in the salutation
	• *Yours faithfully* if you use *Sir or Madam* in the salutation
	✓ Type your full name and sign the letter by hand.
Don'ts	✓ Don't write your name above the address.
	✓ Don't use inappropriate or informal language, e.g. slang, short forms, abbreviations, …

Checklist: Formal letter

Language support	**Say why you are writing:** **to reply:** ✓ In response to your letter of September 23rd … **to complain:** ✓ I am writing to express my dissatisfaction with … ✓ Unfortunately, I am forced to write this letter in order to complain about … **to inquire:** ✓ I am writing to inquire about the possibility of … ✓ I would be very grateful if you would send me further information about … ✓ Would you kindly tell me how …? **to apply:** ✓ I wish to apply for the post of … ✓ I am writing to apply for … ✓ With reference to your advertisement in the Daily News of March 3rd, I should like to apply for the position of … **Say how you expect the recipient to reply to …** **your complaint:** ✓ Under the circumstances, I feel an apology should be offered. ✓ I would be grateful if you could deal with the problem as soon as possible. ✓ I must insist that you refund me my money immediately. **your inquiry:** ✓ I would like to thank you in advance for your assistance. ✓ Please accept my thanks for your help. **your application:** ✓ I look forward to hearing from you. ✓ I will be glad to supply you with any further information you may require. ✓ I have attached / enclosed the following documents.

The example formal letter below details the general layout that your letter should conform to.

The address of the person you are writing to should be on the left.

Say why you are writing the letter in the first paragraph.

In the last part of the letter, say how you expect the recipient to reply.

End the letter in an appropriate way.

> 68, Wood Lane
> Romford RM12 8JY
> sgoodenough@internet.com
>
> November 1, 2015
>
> Ms Diane Poole
> Personnel Department
> Debenhams Ltd.
> Romford RM10 6NX
>
> Dear Ms Poole
>
> With reference to your advertisement in the Romford Recorder of October 24th, I should like to apply for a summer job in your Department Store. My final examinations finish on June 23rd and I will be available to start work any time after that date.
>
> I am just completing my final year at Hornchurch Grammar School and have applied to do Business Studies and French at Bristol University in October. Meanwhile, I would like to gain some experience in a large organisation such as yours, and of course earn some extra money to help finance my university course.
>
> Having worked in a local supermarket on Saturdays for the past two years, I have gained a lot of experience in dealing with customers. I also greatly enjoy working in a team and was always a popular member of any group presentation at school because I always do my share of the work. In my last year at school I was a prefect and also captain of the hockey team, which shows I have a sense of responsibility towards others. My teachers have always considered me to be a reliable and conscientious student.
>
> I have attached my CV and will be glad to supply you with any other information you require, for example, the names of referees. Thank you for considering my application. I look forward to hearing from you soon.
>
> Yours sincerely
> *S. Goodenough*
> Sandra Goodenough

Write your address and email in the top right-hand corner or on the left above the recipient's address.

Leave a line and write the date below your address.

The main part of the letter should include any other necessary information.

Checklist: Speech

When you give a speech, you are aiming to get people to agree with your views. As your speech will only be heard and not read by your audience, you have to be careful how you present what you have to say. Speeches are meant to be spoken, so your language should not be too formal. You may use short forms and contractions like *don't, we're, haven't, I'm,* etc. It may help you to read out aloud to yourself what you have written to check whether your style creates the desired effect.

Dos	**Plan the structure of your speech to include the following parts:** **Introduction:** ✓ Directly address the audience at the beginning. ✓ Begin your introduction with an "attention-getter" to capture your audience's attention, e.g. a story, a rhetorical question, a quotation. ✓ Clearly state the topic of your speech and your personal stance on it. **Main part:** ✓ Explain the topic/problem. ✓ Quote facts and people to persuade your audience. ✓ Show your emotional involvement and appeal to the emotions of the audience. **Conclusion:** ✓ Briefly highlight your main points and end with something strong, e.g. an appeal for support. ✓ Show that the speech has ended, e.g. by thanking your audience for listening.
Don'ts	✓ Don't put too many ideas in your speech, but give the listeners two or three important things to remember. ✓ Don't just read the speech out aloud to your audience. ✓ Don't use too complex expressions. ✓ Don't write very long sentences – listeners must be able to follow you. ✓ Don't use modifiers, e.g. *might be, possibly, probably, more or less,* – you must be very direct and specific to be convincing.
Language support	**Introduction:** ✓ Address the audience: *ladies and gentlemen, fellow students, my friends, members of …, my fellow countrymen, comrades,* etc. **Main part:** ✓ Relate your speech to your listeners. Use receiver-including pronouns and words like *we, us, our, my friends,* etc. ✓ Use connectives to structure your speech: *firstly, finally,* etc. Look at page 141 for help. ✓ Link the different points by using phrases such as: *Having discussed … it is now appropriate to mention …* ✓ Use adverbial phrases to underline your own convictions and win over the audience: *undoubtedly, certainly, undeniably, definitely, indeed, paradoxically, surprisingly, strangely enough, primarily, first and foremost, above all,* etc. ✓ Include rhetorical questions like: *Don't we all agree/want to …?* ✓ Include rhetorical devices like repetitions, exaggerations, alliterations, etc. **Conclusion:** ✓ *Finally, fellow friends of the environment, …* ✓ Clearly indicate the end of your speech: *Thank you for your attention, ladies and gentlemen.*

Checklist: Letter to the editor

Readers of newspapers often write a letter to the editor to comment on something they have read, usually in the hope that the letter will be published in the newspaper. When writing a letter to the editor, take the aspects for writing a formal letter into account. Use formal language, but include strong statements. Before you start writing the letter, you will need to note down important facts and points from the text you are reacting to. Note down any other ideas you have and arrange all of them in a logical order.

Dos	**Introduction:** ✓ Start with *Sir or Madam:* ✓ Leave out any introductory or closing remarks with which you show your politeness or personal interest. Concentrate on the point you are trying to make. ✓ Name the article you refer to at the beginning of your letter. ✓ Give the reason why you are writing the letter, i.e. what you support/criticize/would like to comment on about the article. **Main part:** ✓ Follow a clear line of argumentation and stick to the most important point(s). ✓ Explain why you share or oppose the author's point of view. ✓ Support your arguments with evidence and examples. **Conclusion:** ✓ End with a strong statement that sums up your position and/or says what you expect from future articles on the issue. ✓ Just sign your name and state your place of residence at the end.
Don'ts	✓ Don't use *Dear ...* at the beginning or *Yours sincerely/faithfully* at the end. ✓ Don't quote from the original article unless it is absolutely necessary. ✓ Don't retell the article and explain it to the editor, but explain your view.
Language support	**Starting the letter:** ✓ *I am writing to you in response to the article ...* ✓ *Having read your article ..., I would like to point out ...* ✓ *In your article ..., you claim that ...* ✓ *Your article ... raises the question of whether ...* **Expressing your opinion in the main part of the text:** ✓ *I would like to congratulate you on ...* ✓ *I personally believe that ...* ✓ *I could not have put it better myself.* ✓ *You are absolutely right when you say .../I utterly agree with you that ...* ✓ *I wholeheartedly endorse ...* ✓ *As a firm believer in .../As a supporter of ..., I totally agree/I see no reason why ...* ✓ *Although I understand why ..., I cannot accept your overall conclusion that ...* ✓ *I see your point, but I still feel that ...* ✓ *I think you are mistaken if you believe ...* ✓ *What you need to keep in mind is .../You overlook the fact that ...* ✓ *I would question the argument that ...* **Ending with a strong statement:** ✓ *The question can no longer be whether ..., but ...* ✓ *However, does the evidence I have cited not prove that ...?* ✓ *All in all, there can be no doubt that ...* ✓ *Ultimately, what matters is (that) ...* ✓ *Consequently, I strongly support/oppose your view that ...*

How to work with cartoons

Cartoons are often used to make a critical comment on a serious issue in a humorous way. They are often published in newspapers or magazines. In order to understand the cartoon it is important to look at the details, and you should consider the connection between the picture, the punch line and any speech bubbles.

Issue
Before you study the cartoon in detail, decide what the issue is.

Presentation of characters
Are the characters in the cartoon caricatures of real people like politicians or other persons of public interest, or do they stand for a particular group?

Scene/Setting
What is the situation depicted in the cartoon? Where is it set? Who are the characters involved? What are they doing?

The cat had figured out how to work Ebay.

Source
The cartoon may be published in a newspaper or a magazine. What is the general attitude represented by the paper? Is it more conservative or more liberal? When was the cartoon first published?

Punch line or written comment
Is the punch line presented as direct speech or as a general statement? Does it contain a play on words or a double meaning? Does it suggest a parallel to past or present situations or events?

Language support	
Describing cartoons	Interpreting cartoons
• At the top/bottom of the cartoon … • In the foreground/background … • On the right/left … • In the centre … • In the top/bottom right-hand/left-hand corner … • The cartoonist shows … • There are … in the picture. • The situation reminds one/me/you of … • The cartoon describes …	• The expression on …'s face shows … • The boys are standing close together. This could mean that … • She is hugging him. That suggests … • By presenting …, the cartoonist …

How to quote

When referring to/working with a text, you need quotations from that text to support your statements and findings with evidence.
You can quote directly or indirectly, and you can integrate quotations into your own sentences or quote passages to back up what you have said in your own words.

You may …	Examples
1) … quote indirectly from a text, i.e. say something that can be found in the text in your own words. This is often used when stating facts that need no in-depth interpretation. To show that you haven't quoted directly from the text, use "cf."[1].	Ed works as a taxi driver and plays cards with his friends Audrey and Marvin on a regular basis (cf. p. 58).
2) … integrate direct quotes into your own sentence. But be careful: Don't change the meaning of the quotation, and make sure the resulting sentence is grammatically correct. To show that you are quoting directly from the text, use inverted commas.	Ed comes from one of the parts of the town where the poorer, less educated people live, which he himself describes as a "dirty secret" (p. 59).
3) … quote a short passage or sentence directly to back up what you have already said in your own words. Again, use inverted commas to show that it is a direct quotation.	Ed states clearly that he is not content with his life: "No real career. No respect in the community. Nothing" (p. 58).

When you quote from a text, …

- don't quote very long passages. Quotes should underline or support what you have to say, not say it for you.

- don't use quotes simply to fill paper space – they must refer to your findings.

- quote the exact wording and punctuation from the text. If you leave something out or change something to make it fit into your sentence, you have to indicate that clearly by using […]. You may only make minor changes and mustn't alter the meaning of your quote.

- don't use quotations to retell a text or story.

- make sure the quotes are meaningful – don't quote the first two words followed by "…".

- always refer to lines or pages (l. 1/ll. 5–7/p. 8/pp. 8–9 etc.). Use "l." for one line, "ll." for more than one line, "p." for one page and "pp." for more than one page.

- you should set off the quoted passage further away from the left-hand margin if the quoted text is more than two or three sentences long.

How to improve your text

Once you have written your text, read it carefully again and check whether you have considered the criteria listed below. Revise your text accordingly.

a) **Content:**
- Has your text taken all aspects of the assignment into consideration?
- Have you given evidence to support your arguments?
- Have you referred adequately to the text that has to be analyzed (lines, quotations)?
- Have you avoided repetitions?

b) **Structure and logical order:**
Are the following parts included?
- introduction, introductory sentence
- main part, divided up into several paragraphs
- conclusion

Is the text clearly structured and therefore easy to follow with the help of
- connectives? Look at page 141 for help.
- visible paragraphs?
- a clear order of arguments or examples?

c) **Language and style:**
- Have you used the correct tense, e.g. the simple present tense in a summary?
- Have you used the correct language, e.g. formal language in a letter to the editor?
- Are your sentences complete and not too long or complicated?
- Do appropriate linking words connect ideas and sentences to make your text coherent?
- Have you avoided waffling, i.e. excluded all unnecessary words?
- Have you varied your vocabulary by using synonyms?

> **Language support**
>
> **Synonyms: Improving your style by expressing yourself more precisely (adjectives and nouns)**
> Apart from using sentence links to structure and organize a text, there is another way to improve your style: Simply ban the following from your range of vocabulary – at least when writing a formal text like an analysis or characterization:
>
> SAD   HAPPY   NICE   BAD   INTERESTING   SITUATION
>
> There are various synonyms you might use instead – here are a few examples:
>
> - For "sad" people you could use:
>   *downcast, depressed, downhearted, dejected, dispirited, frustrated, discouraged, sorrowful*
>
> - For "sad" atmosphere you could use:
>   *dark, gloomy, dismal, dreary, depressing, desolate, melancholy, hopeless, cheerless, bleak*
>
> - For "happy" people you could use:
>   *cheerful, contented, relaxed, pleased, delighted, light-hearted, jolly, merry, lively, vivacious, animated, buoyant, humorous, spirited*

- For "nice" people you could use:
  amiable, kind-hearted, good-natured, gentle, congenial, easy-going, pleasant, sympathetic

- For "nice" atmosphere you could use:
  cheerful, relaxed, pleasant, harmonious, idyllic, picturesque, familiar, friendly, warm

- For "bad" people you could use:
  despicable, contemptible, loathsome, hateful, detestable, reprehensible, awful, vile, mean, repulsive, horrible, dreadful, terrible

- For "interesting" you could use:
  appealing, exciting, fascinating, remarkable, significant, captivating, intriguing, attractive

- For "situation" you could use:
  circumstance, case, state of affairs, condition, predicament, position, dilemma

Language support

Writing about the author's opinion, point of view, bias …
When writing about or referring to the author of the text you have to analyze, you should not only write "the author says" but use more precise alternatives instead. Here are several examples of verbs you could use:

The author …

refers to …
alludes to …
talks about/mentions …
addresses the issue of -ing …
examines …
raises the question of whether …

claims/maintains/argues that …
assumes/supposes/presumes that …
asserts …
believes …
states …
insists …
emphasizes …
sides with …
backs up his argument with …
is in favour of -ing …
puts forward another argument …

doubts …
attacks/accuses so. of -ing …
blames sth./so. …
criticizes …
reproaches so. for -ing …
rejects (the idea of) …
abandons the idea of -ing …
opposes the idea of -ing …
refutes the argument …

weighs the arguments …
is in two minds about …

leaves … unanswered …
avoids this issue …
does not consider …

Depending on the type of text you are writing about, there are various synonyms you can use instead of the word "author". Of course, you can also use the author's name or simply "he" or "she".

Synonyms for authors of …

- literary texts: *novelist, playwright, poet, writer*
- newspaper articles: *journalist, reporter, columnist, writer, essayist*

How to structure a text

When analyzing a text or commenting on an issue, you should not only pay attention to the content and the correct use of language (grammar, choice of words, etc.), but also to the structure of your text.

In order to write a well-structured text you should follow the structure of **introduction – main part – conclusion**. Make sure that you plan how to present your ideas effectively in a sequence of paragraphs before you start writing.

Moreover, you should make the relationships between your points clear by using connectives, e.g. to express cause and effect or to point out contrasts and contradictions.

The outline of a text and paragraph writing

Analysis	
Introduction • Refer back to the task, if necessary. • Make a general statement that sums up what you expect to find out.	**Example:** You are asked to write a characterization of the protagonist and give a general assessment of what he is like. *In this extract, which focuses on John's feelings about his parents, John seems to be a highly ambivalent character who pretends to be friendly to his parents on the surface, but in fact hides how much he dislikes his parents.*
Main part • Develop your interpretation/ argumentation in the main part of your analysis/argumentation in a well-structured and logical way so that it is easy for the reader to understand your analysis. • Divide your main part up into meaningful paragraphs before you start writing. • Follow the PEA principle for your paragraph writing. P – point: an introductory sentence that introduces the point that you are trying to make in this paragraph so that the reader immediately knows what you are referring to. E – evidence: examples from the text (including quotations) or arguments and examples that can be used to prove your point (P). A – analysis: the explanation of examples and quotations in order to make it clear how the evidence (E) helps to prove your initial point (P).	**Example:** Characterization of Balram in Adiga's novel "White Tiger": *Judging from his outward appearance, one can initially identify Balram as a typical example of a low-caste servant or a poor Indian in general who slowly becomes aware of the consequences his way of dressing have on his position in society.* (introducing a sequence of paragraphs) *Wearing sandals instead of proper shoes seems to be a distinctive feature separating the rich from the poor in this context as Balram as well as the other drivers all wear sandals. Hence they can identify with the poor man wearing sandals who is refused entry to the shopping mall (cf. ll. 45ff.). As their masters could enter the mall without any problem, Balram and the other drivers realize how the inequality of Indian society manifests itself even in items of clothing.*

Analysis

Conclusion
- Refer back to your opening paragraph.
- Summarize your most important findings concisely.

Example: Characterization of Balram in Adiga's novel "White Tiger":
As a closer look at Balram's character has shown, Balram becomes aware of what makes him recognizable as a lower-caste driver and tries to leave outward appearance as well as other signs like his insufficient command of the English language behind. His new way of dressing, which imitates the style of his master, as well as his recognition that he has to give up old habits that single him out as uneducated and ill-mannered show his determination to rise above his current status.

Comment

Introduction
- Refer back to the task.
   a) If it is a general issue, (example 1), you need to establish a connection to that topic in your opening paragraph.
   b) If you are expected to comment on something that is included in the text you are working on (example 2), you need to refer back to this text.
- Regardless of the context, include a thesis statement which expresses your general view on the issue.

Example 1: You are asked to discuss whether a gap year is worth doing after school.
Thousands of students decide to take a year off from education once they have graduated from school and do not want to start studying straight away. Although this may provide a wide variety of unforgettable experiences, I do not believe that travelling the world for a year is of much benefit for your personal development or your university studies.

Example 2: You are asked to comment on a character's behaviour towards his parents.
As X feels annoyed and humiliated by his parents for not allowing him to live the life of a normal teenager in this situation, it seems highly doubtful that his inability to talk to his parents openly about what bothers him will solve X's problems of unhappiness and isolation.

Comment

Comment	

Main part
• Write your comment in a well-structured way so that it is easy for the reader to follow your line of argumentation.
• Structure your arguments beforehand. There are different patterns:
  • from most to least important argument or the other way round
  • first pros, then cons or the other way round
  • topic-oriented (contrasting pros and cons on the same aspect step by step)
• Follow the PEA principle for your paragraph writing.
P – point: an introductory sentence that introduces the point that you are trying to make in this paragraph so that the reader immediately knows what you are referring to.
E – evidence: examples from the text (including quotations) or arguments and examples that can be used to prove your point (P).
A – analysis: the explanation of examples and quotations in order to make it clear how the evidence (E) helps to prove your initial point (P).
	Example: Discussing how sensible it is to take a year off for a gap year:
	If you choose the place where you are going wisely, you may have the chance to gain some experience in the field you would like to study or work in later. There are definitely some future medical students who assist doctors and nurses in some developing country or those who want to study science and help out in a bird sanctuary or get involved in an environmental project, for example. However, the question is whether everyone already has a clear idea of what they would like to do after their gap year and would maybe prefer to use the year to make up their minds. Even if they would like to gain some experience in the field that interests them, they might not be able to find a suitable place.

Conclusion • Refer back to your opening paragraph. • Draw a conclusion by weighing up the pros and cons in your argumentation.	**Example:** Discussing how sensible it is to take a year off for a gap year: *All in all, I'm utterly convinced that gap years do not really allow you to acquire new skills and prepare for university. Although it may serve as a character-building experience to become more independent and able to adapt to new people and circumstances, I doubt that many situations you experience while travelling around the world are realistic and that these experiences can be applied to everyday life back home. Consequently, I would never do a gap year, but would rather go abroad as part of my degree course.*

How to structure a text

Expressing connections between points in the text

Language support	
Adding and ordering points:	• To begin with/First of all/Firstly, … • Secondly, …/Then … • Last but not least … • Finally/In the end , … • All in all/To conclude/To sum up … • The most important point is/Above all … • This also becomes evident when …/… during/… in a scene • Both … and …/… not only …, but also … • This assumption can be supported by … • This is also shown by … • Another point/Another example of … is … • In addition to that/Additionally/Furthermore/Moreover/Besides/On top of that, …
Expressing a contrast:	• In spite of the fact …/Despite the fact … • Whereas … • In contrast to … , … • However, … • But nevertheless, … • On the one hand …, on the other hand … • Although …/Even though …/Even if … • While it is true that …, …
Expressing cause and effect:	• Due to …/Because of …/As a result of … • Therefore, …/For this reason, … • … because … • As/Since … • So/Thus …/Accordingly, … • As a consequence, …/Consequently, …/This results in …
Summing up:	• All in all, …/To sum up, …/As a result, … • In brief, …/In conclusion, …/To conclude, …

How to work with a dictionary

All competences, but especially reading and writing, often involve the use of a dictionary. There are **monolingual dictionaries**, which provide definitions in English and **bilingual dictionaries**, which give you the German equivalents. Most of the time you will be using a bilingual dictionary.

English – German

When working with texts you may not always understand all the words, so you will need to refer to a dictionary. The use of the dictionary, however, may be determined by the situation you are in.

- Don't look up every single word you don't know but apply the **strategie**s you have learnt **to understand words from the context** first.
- **Limit the number of words to look up** as using the dictionary is quite time-consuming.
- Depending on the task you are given it may be necessary to **check all the words you don't understand**. If you read a novel or a longer text of course, you will need to use your strategies of understanding words from the context, from cognates etc. But sometimes you need to get a detailed understanding of the text.
- Having gone to the trouble of finding the word, try and use it to build and **extend your active vocabulary**.
  - Decide if the word may be useful for later use.
  - Collect the words you have selected in word fields.
  - Add collocations or idioms to avoid possible mistakes in future.
  - Use the newly acquired words and phrases in your homework/written texts. This is the best way to remember them.

How to look the word up properly

- Make sure you look the word up in its **correct spelling** or you may end up with an incorrect translation. Examples of this are: *board-bored, fair-fare, sail-sale*.
- Determine whether the word you are looking up is a noun, a verb, an adjective etc. and read the corresponding part of the entry. With verbs, make sure you look for the basic form.
- There may still be different meanings. Read the complete entry and decide which translation fits the context of your text best.
- Avoid mistakes by checking what grammatical construction is needed with the word you want to use, for example *used to **do*** as opposed to *get used to **doing***.

The phonetic transcription shows you how to pronounce a word correctly. It not only reflects the sound but also gives you the intonation of a word, which may be different depending on the function of the word (e.g. pre'sent *v* – 'present *n*).

n, vi, vt, adj tell you what type of word it is (noun, verb etc.). If there are abbreviations you don't understand, check the explanations in the dictionary.

The headword helps you to find the word more easily.

chest [tʃest] *n* **1.** *(torso)* Brust *f*, Brustkorb *m*; **to fold one's arm across one's ~** die Arme vor der Brust verschränken – **2.** *(trunk)* Truhe; *(box)* Kiste – **3.** *(treasury)* Schatzkästchen

The different meanings of a word are listed under numbers. Make sure that you read the whole entry to find the meaning that fits the context.

Expressions in bold letters give you examples of how to use the word correctly in typical phrases or idioms (e.g. "heavy: ~ accent, with a ~ heart").

German – English

When writing texts you will with time want to make your phrasing more precise, varied and differentiated.

Typical needs

- **Spelling:** You are not sure how the English word you want to use is written.
  - Check for changes in spelling in different grammatical contexts.

- **Vocabulary:** You want to use a particular word.
  - Make sure you have the correct German spelling. For example: The word *Widerspruch* will be hard to find if you think it is spelt with *ie*.
  - Read through **all** the possible meanings and consider the specific lexical area in which you want to use the word. For example: The German word *Bank* can mean either *bank* or *bench* in English.
  - If collocations are given, try to use the whole phrase or a parallel construction in your own text.

- **Style: variation (synonyms/antonyms):** When writing a text and editing it you will find that you have repeated certain words.
  - Use the definitions of the German word you have looked up to find other ways in English of expressing it.

Internet dictionaries

/dict.leo.org/
/www.dict.cc/

It may seem the quickest route to use an Internet dictionary, but this often is the quickest way to making lots of mistakes: Internet dictionaries often offer a one-to-one translation which may not always fit. So don't go for the first option but check carefully in which context the respective word can be used.

Tip: Since you will have to work with a non-digital dictionary in your exams, you should practise working with one in class and at home.
  - You will start to get quicker at finding words.
  - You will start to get more confident in choosing the right meaning.
  - You will get used to benefitting from the additional information the dictionary offers you.

How to give feedback / peer-edit

Giving constructive feedback is a helpful way of improving the quality of your own and of your classmates' work.

Feedback on a presentation

Make sure that the feedback you give …
- is worded in such a way that your classmates can accept it without being embarrassed.
- is objective and not personal.
- focuses more on the corrected form and does not dwell on the mistake.
- highlights the use of good language.

Language support	
Here are some phrases you can use to give positive feedback on a presentation by your classmates:	• What I really liked was that you … • What really impressed me was … • I particularly liked … • I think it was a good idea to … • You managed to …
If you need to be more critical, these expressions can help you:	• The explanations/facts given were not (quite) correct. • What could be improved is … • I would have liked to learn more about … • I missed information about … • You did not manage to …

Peer-editing

A good method of improving your writing is peer-editing. It means working with someone from your class to help you to improve, revise and edit each other's writing.

When editing a text check the following aspects:

- **Topic:** Check whether the writer stays on the topic. Information that is not relevant should be left out.

- **Choice of words:** Make sure the writer uses interesting words and not too many "overused" words (e.g. *really, very, nice, interesting*). A writer should also use language which is appropriate for the relevant text type (e.g. register, thematic vocabulary, etc.).

- **Sentences:** Check for sentences that are either too long or too short. A good writer also uses linking words to join his/her sentences.

- **Structure of the text:** A good text should be well organized and easy to understand. An introduction should immediately grab a reader's attention.

How to give feedback / peer-edit

When peer editing a text, you should keep three aspects in mind:

- **Compliments:** The most important rule of peer editing is to BE POSITIVE! Always start with compliments. Remember, you are helping to improve someone else's work. First tell the writer what you think he/she did well. Here are some phrases you can use to give positive feedback:
  This was fun to read because …
  I liked the way you …
  My favourite part was … because …
  I think you used a lot of good details.

- **Suggestions:** Make suggestions by giving some specific ideas about how to improve the piece of writing. Remember to try and stay positive and always try to provide constructive criticism. For example:
  Don't say to your partner: *This paragraph doesn't make any sense.*
  Tell him/her: *If you add more details after this sentence, it will be clearer.*
  Rather than saying: *Your choice of words was boring*, say: *Instead of using the word 'good', maybe you can use the word 'exceptional'.*

- **Corrections:** Only after you and your partner have agreed on how to change your pieces of writing can you actually start with the final step in the peer editing process: making corrections.
  Swap your texts and check your partner's work for
    - spelling mistakes
    - grammar mistakes
    - missing punctuation

Here is some advice on how to spot mistakes:
- Read the text more than once and concentrate on one aspect at a time, e.g. spelling mistakes.
- If you have typed your text on the computer, use the spellchecker in Word.
- After you have finished writing your text, take a break before you check it for mistakes.
- Reading "backwards", i.e. from end to beginning, might do the trick to spot mistakes.

How to improve your mediation skills

You are very likely to be confronted with situations where people who do not speak German need your help because some information they need is only available in German. Such situations are very similar to those that you find in mediation tasks.

Step 1: Understanding the task

Before you start working on a mediation task, make sure that you fully understand what is required from you. Mediation does not mean translating the German original word for word.

a) What is the type of text you need to produce?

In the example below, you can see that the German original is an interview, but the text you should produce is a newspaper article. So you must change the way the information is presented to you in German. In order to do this, you need to remember what is typical of that particular kind of text. In the case of a newspaper article, you should remember to include a headline, start with an interesting introduction, write a main part and finish with a final part/conclusion.

> Die Internetseite UK-German Connection Voyage, die deutsche und britische Jugendliche einander näherbringen möchte, unterhält ein Onlinemagazin, in dem junge Deutsche und Briten Artikel vor allem über das Verhältnis beider Völker veröffentlichen können.
> Sie sind eingeladen, einen kurzen Zeitungsartikel über die Gemeinsamkeiten und Unterschiede zwischen deutschem und englischem Humor und Umgang mit Sprache zu verfassen. Als Grundlage nutzen Sie ein Zeitungsinterview mit zwei Journalisten aus Deutschland und Großbritannien, die im jeweils anderen Land leben und arbeiten.

b) What information is needed?

Read the task carefully to find out what information is needed. Certain passages or elements of the German text are likely to be irrelevant to the task. You can leave this information out in your version.

c) Who is the addressee?

In a mediation task, another factor that should influence the way you deal with the text is the addressee that is mentioned in the task. If you write a text for teenagers, your text should be less formal and technical than if you were writing about a difficult topic for experts in a particular field, for example.

Step 2: Working on the task

a) Reading

- Highlight all the information relevant to the task (see Step 1b).
- Make notes in English.
- Do not get stuck looking for a literal translation of a German expression. Sometimes it doesn't exist and you can paraphrase the idea you want to express. For example, there may be a German idiomatic expression like "das Zeitliche segnen" which you cannot translate directly. So you need to find either an English idiom that has a similar meaning or go for a more neutral expression, for example "to die".

b) Writing the English text

- Arrange the information you highlighted and noted down in a logical order that fits the type of text you are expected to write. Structure it in such a way that it is easy to understand for the people who are supposed to read your text.
- As stated above, you needn't translate the German text word for word. It is important that all the relevant information is presented clearly. Leave out anything that is not related to the task, but also leave out any personal comments unless you are invited to do so by the task.
- Be careful with expressions and concepts that are very specific to German and Germany. You may have to include an explanation to someone from abroad. For example, a text may include references to people or institutions that most Germans know, but people from abroad do not know. So you need to add a short explanation: *Most Germans watch <u>the news programme</u> "Tagesschau" at 8 o'clock at night on ARD, <u>which is a public TV channel.</u>*

c) Editing the text

- Make sure that you have included all the relevant information required by the task and not used anything that goes beyond it.
- Check that your text fits the criteria of the type of text that the task has asked you to produce.
- Don't forget that the style and register of the text must suit the addressees that the text is intended for. If necessary, make some changes to style and register.
- Check your text for grammatical correctness and the right choice of words.

How to improve your oral skills

Monologue

Oral exams may have different types of assignments that require a monologue. You may be confronted with texts, pictures, cartoons, role cards, statistics or a film sequence and you may be asked to
- summarize a text
- describe and analyze a text or visuals or
- give a presentation prepared at home.

Apart from the content of your statements your language competence will be evaluated.
So it is important that you
- extend your topical vocabulary to make your statements concise and clear which means that you should work on thematic vocabulary lists during course work.
- make sure you pronounce words correctly, so check the pronunciation of new words as you come across them.
- avoid basic grammar mistakes.
- use connectives to link your sentences and make your monologue more fluent.

Phrases that open up a new range of ideas or structure your presentation
may be especially helpful:

furthermore, what is more, besides, in addition,
generally speaking, on the whole,
basically, interestingly, surprisingly
as I said before,
considering those facts/character traits/the author's intention/the author's arguments

It is important to use your presentation time to note down important aspects that you would like to mention in your talk. So highlight words or phrases in a given text, write ideas in the margin and/or list the aspects that seem relevant to you in the order you want to present them. You can use your notes as cue cards during the presentation.

Language support		
To start your talk or presentation you can use the following phrases:	To structure your talk the following phrases may be helpful:	To conclude your presentation you could use phrases like:
• First I'm going to talk about … • I would like to start by … • To begin with, let me describe … • First of all I want to say …	• Secondly … • Next I'd like to point out … • Another important argument is … • On the one hand … on the other hand	• Finally … • To sum up, one could say that … • All things considered, I would say that …

Dialogue

The second part of your exam will be a conversation, either with your teacher or with one or more fellow students.
This situation will test your communicative skills.
So it is important that you are able to do the following:

Language support	
State your view clearly and think of alternative phrases for *I think*.	• I believe that … • I'm convinced that … • I would say that … • In my view … • In my opinion … • As far as I'm concerned …
Clarify your view if necessary.	• What I mean is … • That's not exactly what I mean. • To put it in other words / in other words …
Ask for clarification if you are not sure you know exactly what the other person means.	• Do you (really) mean that …? • I'm not sure I fully understand what you mean. • Does that mean that …? • When you say …, do you mean …?
Use a variety of phrases to agree and disagree in a polite way.	• That's exactly how I see it. • I would say so, too. • I completely agree. • Do you really think so? • I wouldn't say so. • Well, I'm not totally convinced. • You may be right but … • I see your point but …
Use conversational gambits that signal your view but also give you time to think.	• well / sure / definitely / absolutely / exactly / quite / well, perhaps … • I see / Let me see / I know / so?
Involve your partner and bring him/her back into the conversation.	• Well, that's my view. So what do you think? • What makes you so sure? • Don't you think that …? • It's obvious that …, isn't it? • Wouldn't you say so?

How to analyze statistics

Statistics can appear in different forms. Usually, they take one of the forms below:

bar chart

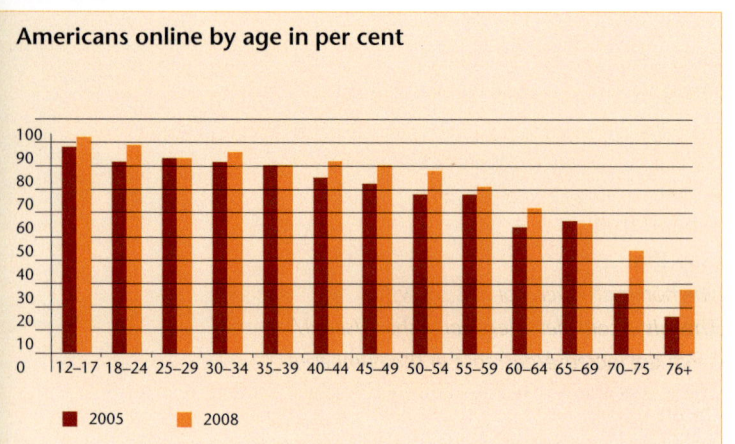

Americans online by age in per cent

(2005, 2008 by age groups: 12–17, 18–24, 25–29, 30–34, 35–39, 40–44, 45–49, 50–54, 55–59, 60–64, 65–69, 70–75, 76+)

pie chart

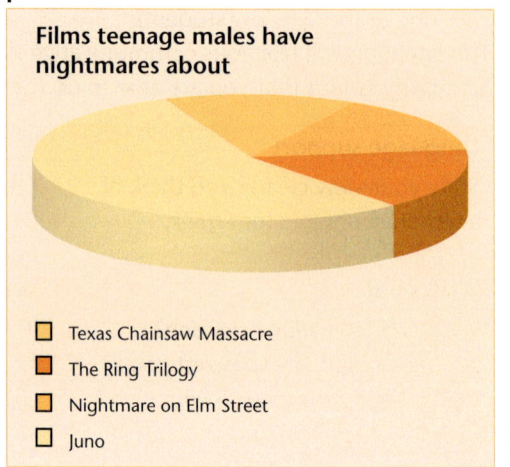

Films teenage males have nightmares about

- Texas Chainsaw Massacre
- The Ring Trilogy
- Nightmare on Elm Street
- Juno

line graph

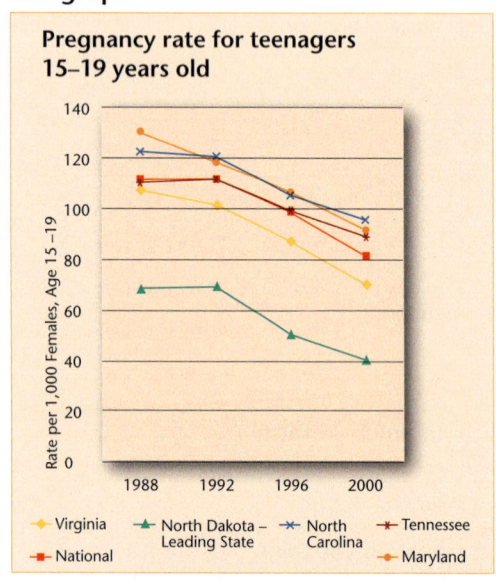

Pregnancy rate for teenagers 15–19 years old

Rate per 1,000 Females, Age 15–19 (1988, 1992, 1996, 2000)

- Virginia
- North Dakota – Leading State
- North Carolina
- Tennessee
- National
- Maryland

table

Teen unemployment in the US

Year	All Teens	White Teens	Black Teens	Hispanic Teens	All Workers
2001	14.7%	12.7%	29.0%	17.7%	4.7%
2002	16.5	15.5	29.8	20.1	5.8
2003	17.5	15.2	33.0	20.0	6.0
2004	17.0	15.0	31.7	20.4	5.5
2005	16.6	14.2	33.3	18.4	5.1
2006	15.4	13.2	29.1	15.9	4.6
2007	15.7	13.9	29.4	18.1	4.6
2008	18.7	16.8	31.2	22.4	5.8
2009	24.3	21.8	29.5	30.2	9.3
2010	25.9	23.2	43.0	32.2	9.6
2011	26.3	23.5	46.9	32.9	9.0

Studying the figures

1. Before you start analyzing statistics, make sure you study the graph/chart/table carefully. Find out what the statistics are about.

2. Study the legend and the figures and check if they are absolute numbers or percentages. Pay special attention to the way the figures are presented visually to make sure that proportions are represented accurately, for example.

3. Look for general trends or noteworthy figures or correlations. What you can find out depends largely on the type of visualisation. Pie charts and bar graphs usually deal with the relative size/importance of data, line graphs and tables often emphasize certain developments including peaks and troughs in trends.

How to analyze statistics

Describing and interpreting the figures

Introduction:	
• How are the figures presented? • What is the graph/chart/table about? • What is the source of the figures?	The graph/chart/table shows/presents/provides information on/deals with …, covering a period of … The topic/subject/theme of the graph/chart/table is … It is taken from/The source of the data is … The graph/chart/table was published by …
Description:	
• How do the figures develop? • What is the highest/lowest point? • What are the most striking points? • Are there any irregular figures? • If there are figures to compare, are there any similarities/differences?	The horizontal/vertical axis shows … There is a considerable/steady/sharp/slight/marked increase/decrease in the number of … The number/amount/proportion of … has changed slightly/clearly … The numbers drop/fall/decrease … The figures remain constant/steady … The figures reach a peak/a trough in … In …, X bottomed out at 8%/peaked out at 32%. The average figure for … is … The pie is subdivided into segments that represent … The chart/graph/table reveals/shows that … The numbers for … are about twice as high as those … The … with the highest frequency/number of … is …
Conclusion and evaluation:	
• What general conclusion can be drawn from the figures? • What could be reasons for the figures? • How can the figures be related to each other? • What can be predicted on the basis of those figures? • How do the figures relate to what you know about the topic? Are they objective or biased?	All in all/By and large, the statistics for … reveal/show/… that … It seems likely/unlikely that the figures for … will (not) continue to … Against the background of …, the figures/results are (not) very surprising/revealing/enlightening … The data confirm/contradict/are (not) consistent with … The graph/chart/table conveys a false/one-sided impression because …

How to listen effectively

Learning a foreign language properly is impossible without learning to listen effectively. Listening comprehension tasks, however, can take very different forms as you may have to listen to a dialogue/interview, a speech, a song, etc. The situations , e.g. parliament, family context, vary as much as the accents, tempo, etc. of the speakers.

a) Preparing for a listening comprehension

Before you start listening, you should make use of all the information that you may already have about what you are going to listen to. So make sure you read the task carefully. Think about the topic you have been discussing in class. If there are photos, headings, additional texts, study them so that you already have some ideas of what the listening text may be about.

b) Listening strategies

- When you listen to an audio clip for the first time, listen for gist, i.e. the main ideas (who?, what?, why?, etc.). Key words that are repeated several times may help you work out what the text is about.
- While listening to the text for the first time, keep the task in mind and try to remember when in the clip there are relevant passages you should concentrate on when you listen to it for the second time.
- Do not try to understand every single word, but the general message. If you listen to a clip a second or even a third time, you will notice that you understand more and more. You will then be able to work out the meaning of words from the context or from similarities they have to other words you know from English (e.g. *high – height*, *clean – cleanliness*), German or another language (e.g. *deny so. sth.* – French: *dénier*).

c) Working on the tasks

- Use a pencil to take notes or, if it is a multiple-choice test, mark the correct answers.
- Add to your notes when you listen again.
- If it is not a test, check with your neighbour to see if you understood the same things.

Glossary – Literary terms

literary terms	definition	example
non-fiction	**texts that give facts about real events, things or people**	
bias	a prejudice in favour of or against one thing, person or group. It is a tendency to hold a certain point of view at the expense of other alternatives. An article is biased if information is presented in a one-sided way based on personal opinion rather than facts.	
caption	words printed near or on a picture that explain sth. about the picture; a joke that is printed underneath a humorous drawing or photograph	
conclusion/ concluding paragraph	the final part of an article or a piece of writing	
ellipsis	leaving out words to avoid repetition	"Anyone's guess."
enumeration	naming each one of a series or list of things	
euphemism	a word or expression that people use when they want to talk about something unpleasant or embarrassing without mentioning the thing itself. It is used to spare the reader's feelings.	"to kick the bucket", "to fall off one's perch", "to pop one's clogs" are euphemisms of 'to die'.
exaggeration	representing (sth.) as being larger, greater, better, or worse than it really is	"We've heard this complaint a thousand times."
headline	the title of a cartoon, a newspaper story, etc.	
imagery	use of vivid or descriptive language to represent objects, actions or ideas	"The rich, dark soil of our land became red with our blood."
introduction	the part at the beginning of any text	
irony	a literary style employing contrasts for humorous or rhetorical effect	"In fact, it was his last big joke before his sense of humour calcified and had to be removed."
litotes	understatement making sth./so. less important than in reality	"She's not as young as she was." = She's old.
main part/body	the body/main part of a book or document, not including the introduction or the notes	
metaphor	two ideas that are normally not linked are compared in a metaphor without using "as" or "like". This creates an image in the reader's mind and makes the description more powerful.	"They blazed a trail toward freedom through the darkest of nights." (Barack Obama)
paradox	a statement consisting of two parts that seem to mean the opposite of each other	"I can't resist anything but temptation." (Oscar Wilde)
paragraph	a section of a piece of writing that begins on a new line and contains a group of several interrelated sentences	
parallelism	the repetition of sentence pattern often used to contrast	
personification	the presentation of ideas, objects or animals as persons to make them more interesting for the reader	"That carrot cake with the cream cheese icing is calling my name."

Literary terms – non-fiction/novel

literary terms	definition	example
point of view	the relation in which the narrator stands to the story, a mental viewpoint or attitude	
register	the level of language (degree of formality)	formal, informal, slang, …
repetition	words or phrases that are used more than once in a text, catching the reader's attention	"She knew this though: she loved kites and she loved rainbows. And, above all, she loved her mother."
rhetorical question	a question which expects no answer	"What does it matter now?"
simile	a comparison of two ideas, often linked by "as" or "like"	"Like a magic kingdom that belonged only to Grace and her mother."
structure	the organisation of the elements of a text	
style	the special, often personal and individual way in which a writer expresses ideas depending on personal factors and the type of text he/she is writing	
stylistic devices	techniques used to convince the reader/listener of the author's idea	repetition, enumeration, irony, exaggeration, metaphor, tone, …
sub-heading	the title of one section of a longer piece of writing	
subtext	the hidden meaning in a conversation, not expressed by words, but by intonation, tone of voice, facial expression, gesture, posture	
theme	the main idea the writer usually wants to present. As the theme is usually not stated directly, the reader has to figure it out.	
tone	the tone the author uses to convey his/her attitude towards the subject	ironic, sarcastic, serious, sentimental, humorous, …

novel	a fairly long fictional prose narrative. Normally it has a plot which develops through actions, speech, and thoughts of its characters.	
action	everything that happens in a fictional text; events that form part of a play or film	In this scene, the action takes place in …
allusion	a reference to a familiar or famous historical literary figure	
antagonist	the main character in opposition to the protagonist of a novel	
anti-hero	a main character in a novel or drama who does not have the qualities that a hero usually has, such as idealism or being morally good	
atmosphere	the feeling or mood created by the author through the description of events, setting, situation, etc.	"For a moment, a cloud drifted past the moon and the sky turned greenish gray."
character	a person who takes part in the action of a fictional text	Katniss Everdeen in Suzanne Collins' 'The Hunger Games'

Literary terms – novel

literary terms	definition	example
characterization	the way in which a writer creates characters in a book, play, film, etc. The author may present his characters in two ways: directly by describing them (explicit), or indirectly through their actions, thoughts or feelings and words (implicit).	"I was too lazy at school." "Audrey always sits opposite me, no matter where we play." → She seems to be interested.
climax/ crisis	the most exciting or important moment in a story, event, or situation, usually near the end. This moment determines whether the situation will improve or grow worse. *Crisis* refers to the highest point of reader interest.	
dénouement	the last part of a short story, book, play, etc. in which everything is settled	
dynamic character	a complex character who may change (= round character)	Manjit in Bali Rai's '(Un)arranged marriage'
explicit characterization	direct characterization by the narrator (telling). The author tells the reader explicitly about the character's looks, traits, attitudes.	"He was so bloody thick it was like talking to a gorilla sometimes."
exposition	the first part in a fictional text that provides background information and introduces the setting, the conflict and often the main character or character(s)	
external action	the writer describes what the characters do	"Just as the clock strikes two, the mayor steps up to the podium and begins to read."
falling action	the part of a story or play following the crisis/climax and leading to the dénouement or catastrophe	
flat character	a character who does not develop in the course of the action and is often a stereotype (= static character)	Effie Trinket in Susanne Collins' 'The Hunger Games'
foreshadowing	the technique of hinting at future events in such a way that the reader/viewer is preapred for them or can even anticipate them	
hero/heroine	the main character, protagonist, who usually has good qualities	
implicit characterization	indirect characterization through action, behaviour, words, feelings and thoughts (showing). You learn a lot about a character by studying what he says and does, how he behaves in certain situations and interacts with others.	"Audrey always sits opposite me, no matter where we play." → She seems to be interested.
internal action	the writer shows the thoughts and feelings of the characters	
irony	→ *see non-fiction, p. 153*	
metaphor	→ *see non-fiction, p. 153*	
mood	the feeling that the writer tries to evoke	anger, excitement, happiness, sadness, pity, …
narrative	any writing that tells a story	
narrator	a fictitious person who tells the story in a novel or film	

Literary terms – novel

literary terms	definition	example
omniscient narrator	a narrator knowing everything about the characters	
open ending	a structural element in ficitonal texts in which the conflict remains for the most part unresolved	
paragraph	→ see non-fiction, p. 153	
perspective	the point of view from which a story is presented. The story can be told by a first-person or by a third-person narrator. The narrator can be in or outside the story. The third-person narrator can be omniscient (knowing everything about the characters) or limited (perceiveing and knowing the same things as one character, seeing through the eyes of one character).	first-person perspective third-person perspective: omniscient or limited
plot	a series of related events that make up the main story in a book, film, etc.	
point of view	→ see non-fiction, p. 154	
protagonist	the main character in a fictional text	Winston Smith in George Orwell's '1984'
register	→ see non-fiction, p. 154	
repetition	→ see non-fiction, p. 154	
rhetorical question	→ see non-fiction, p. 154	
rising action	the part of a fictional text following the exposition and leading to the climax/turning point	
round character	a complex character who may change (= dynamic character)	Manjit in Bali Rai's '(Un)arranged marriage'
setting	the place and time at which the action of a fictional text takes place	
simile	→ see non-fiction, p. 154	
static character	a character who does not develop in the course of the action and is often a stereotype (= flat character)	Effie Trinket in Suzanne Collins' 'The Hunger Games'
stream of consciousness	the thoughts of a character in a book that are expressed as they happen	
structure	→ see non-fiction, p. 154	
sub-plot	a plot that is subordinate to the main plot of a literary work	
subtext	→ see non-fiction, p. 154	
suspense	a feeling of excitement or worry that makes a reader curious about the outcome of a fictional text	
symbol	an image that does not only stand for itself but also signifies a more abstract concept or idea	
tension	the feeling evoked by conflicts of a fictional text	

Literary terms – novel/cartoons/non-fictional texts

literary terms	definition	example
theme	the main idea the writer wants to present. As the theme is usually not stated directly, the reader has to figure it out.	
tone	→ see non-fiction, p. 154	
turning point	the point at which the action takes a different, often unexpected direction	

cartoons/non-fictional texts		
bias	→ see non-fiction, p. 153	
caption	→ see non-fiction, p. 153	
caricature	a presentation in which so.'s/sth.'s features are exaggerated to produce a comic or grotesque effect	
euphemism	→ see non-fiction, p. 153	
exaggeration	representing (sth.) as being larger, greater, better, or worse than it really is	"We've heard this complaint a thousand times."
focal point	the central point in a cartoon which is of interest	
headline	the title of a cartoon, a newspaper story, etc.	
introduction	→ see non-fiction, p. 153	
irony	→ see non-fiction, p. 153	
litotes	→ see non-fiction, p. 153	
non-fiction	texts that give facts about real events, things or people	
paradox	→ see non-fiction, p. 153	
personification	→ see non-fiction, p. 153	
point of view	→ see non-fiction, p. 154	
register	→ see non-fiction, p. 154	
rhetorical question	→ see non-fiction, p. 154	
subtext	→ see non-fiction, p. 154	
symbol	→ see novel, p. 156	
tone	→ see non-fiction, p. 154	

Literary terms – novel/cartoons/non-fictional texts/film

literary terms	definition	example
film	a series of moving pictures with sound that you can watch at the cinema or on television	
acoustic effects	effects relating to sound, e.g. in a play or a film	
action	everything that happens in a fictional text; events that form part of a play or film	In this scene, the action takes place in …
actor/actress	the person who performs in a play or film	Jesse Eisenberg as Mark Zuckerberg in 'The Social Network'
anti-hero	→ see novel, p. 154	
atmosphere	→ see novel, p. 154	
backlighting	filming a subject or object illuminated from behind	
cameraman	so. who operates a camera for making films or TV programmes	
cast	noun: all the performers in a play or film verb: to choose an actor for a role in a play or film	
characterization	→ see novel, p. 155	
climax/crisis	→ see novel, p. 155	
close-up	a full-screen shot of a person's face to show emotions revealed by their facial expression; it can also be used to draw attention to an object that is of particular interest to the plot or has a symbolic function	
composer	so. who writes the music, e.g. for a film	
crane shot	the camera is placed on a crane and moves in all directions. A crane is generally used for high angle shots.	
credits	a list of people involved in the making of a film	
cross-cutting (parallel action)	combining shots of two or more scenes which are usually taking place at the same time	
cut	a quick move from one shot to the next in a film	
dialogue	the words that characters speak in a fictional text, play or film	
director (filmmaker)	so. who is in charge of making a film, or getting a play ready for performance, instructs the actors and the crew	David Fincher ('The Social Network')
director of photography	so. who is responsible for setting up the camera and lighting the shot	
editing (montage)	the arrangement of shots in a structured sequence	
establishing shot	gives an overall impression of the location at the beginning of a scene	
exposition	the first part of a fictional text that provides background information and introduces the setting, the conflict and often the main character or character(s)	

Literary terms – film

literary terms	definition	example
extreme close-up (detail shot)	shows an object in detail, emphasizing its importance in the scene	
fade-in	if a sound or picture fades in, it gradually becomes louder or clearer	
fade-out	if a sound or picture fades out, it gradually disappears	
field size (camera range)	the distance between the camera and the object filmed	
flashback	a scene that shows what happened in the past and thus interrupts the chronological order of the plot	
flashforward	a scene that shows what may happen in the future and thus interrupts the chronological order of the plot	
format	a term used to describe the genre of a film or television programme	
full shot	gives a view of the entire figure of a person to show action or to give an impression of a constellation of characters	
hand-held camera (handy cam)	the cameraman holds the camera in his hand when filming. This conveys a feeling of authenticity to the viewer.	
hero/heroine	the main character, protagonist, who usually has good qualities	
high angle shot	the camera looks down on the object so that it seems smaller, less important or inferior	
jump cut	a cut between two pictures leaving out some action	
lighting	refers to the illumination of a camera subject being filmed. The lighting may be natural or artificial, very bright (high-key lighting) or dark (low-key lighting).	
long shot	provides a view of the situation or setting from a distance	
low angle shot	the camera looks up at a person so that people seem more important, powerful or even intimidating as it shows them in a superior position	
match cut	two scenes that are connected by visual or acoustic means. e.g. a door is closed in one scene and opened in the following scene in a different context, someone is crying at the end of the first and the beginning of the second scene	
medium long shot	shows a person or people in interaction with their surroundings	

Literary terms – film

literary terms	definition
medium shot	shows a person down to the waist, often used to present two people in conversation
mood	the feeling that the writer tries to evoke, such as excitement, anger, sadness, happiness, pity, etc.
overhead shot (bird's eye view)	makes an object seem less important, or gives orientation
over-the-shoulder shot	often used to present two people in conversation. You are looking straight at one person from behind the second person
pace	the speed at which sth. happens or is done
pan (panning shot)	the camera moves horizontally, i.e. to the left or to the right as opposed to tilting
perspective	→ see novel, p. 156
plot	a series of related events that make up the main story in a book, film, etc.
point of view	→ see non-fiction, p. 154
point-of-view shot	assumes the perspective of one of the characters so that we seem to look through his/her eyes
producer	the person who is responsible for the financing and marketing of a film
production designer	the person who designs the set for scenes that are shot in the studio
reverse-angle shot	a sequence of point-of-view shots in which the perspective changes from one speaker to the other
scene	a part of an act in a play or film in which events happen in the same place or period of time
script (screenplay)	a written description of the dialogue and action of a play or film, including basic camera or stage directions
scriptwriter	the person who writes the text for a film
sequence	a series of scenes which belong together
setting	the place and time at which the action of a fictional text takes place
shot	a length of film without a break; the smallest structural unit of a film

Literary terms – film

literary terms	definition	example
sound designer	the person who creates special sounds for a film	
sound recordist	the person who records the dialogue spoken by the actors	
sound technician	the person in charge of a film's soundtrack	
soundtrack	all the recorded sound of a film (dialogue, sound and sound effects)	
special effect	an unusual image or sound that has been produced artificially	
static shot	the camera does not move	
still	a photograph taken from one of the scenes in a film	
storyboard	a series of pictures that the director of a film uses to plan the action that will be filmed	
straight-on angle (eye-level shot)	the camera looks straight at the person: this may suggest a neutral view, however, it can also mean that two people who are not on the same level for some reason (e.g. wealth, age, academic standing, social class) are presented as equal to each other.	
sub-plot	a plot that is subordinate to the main plot of a literary work	
subtext	→ see non-fiction, p. 154	
suspense	a feeling of excitement or worry that makes a reader curious about the outcome of a fictional text	
synchronisation	the technique of matching the sound with the image	
tension	the feeling evoked by the conflicts of a fictional text	
tilt (tilting shot)	the camera moves vertically, i.e. upwards or downwards as opposed to panning	
tracking shot	the camera follows a person or an object	
trailer	a short filmed advertisement for a film	
transcript	the storyboard and the complete dialogue of a film	
turning point	the point at which the action takes a different, often unexpected direction	
voice-on	the speaker is not shown in the picture	
voice-off	the speaker is shown in the picture	
voice-over	the voice of a narrator commenting on what is being shown	
zoom in/zoom out	a stationary camera seems to move closer to or further away from the object, thus focussing on it or showing it in its surroundings	

Literary terms – drama

literary terms	definition	example
drama	a work in prose or verse presenting a story which normally deals with human conflict. It is usually intended to be acted on a stage as a play.	
act	one of the parts that a play is divided into. Each act is divided into two or more scenes.	Act I, scene II
acting time	the time the action of a narrative lasts as opposed to reading time	
action	everything that happens in a fictional text; events that form part of a play or film	In this scene, the action takes place in …
actor/actress	→ see film, p. 158	
antagonist	→ see novel, p. 154	
anti-hero	→ see novel, p. 154	
atmosphere	→ see novel, p. 154	
cast	noun: all the performers in a play or film verb: to choose an actor for a role in a play or film	
catastrophe	the unfortunate end of a story	
character	a person who takes part in the action of a fictional text	
characterization	→ see novel, p. 155	
climax/crisis	the most exciting or important moment in a story, event, or situation, usually near the end. This moment determines whether the situation will improve or grow worse. *Crisis* refers to the highest point of reader interest.	
comic relief	a humorous scene or incident in a serious play that relieves the tension	
conflict	the disagreement between opposing forces which is the basis of the plot of a play	
dénouement	the last part of a short story, book, play, etc. in which everything is settled	
dialogue	the words that characters speak in a fictional text, play or film	
dynamic character	→ see novel, p. 155	
exposition	the first part in a fictional text that provides background information and introduces the setting, the conflict and often the main character or character(s)	
falling action	the part of a story or play following the crisis/climax and leading to the dénouement or catastrophe	
flat character	→ see novel, p. 155	
foreshadowing	the technique of hinting at future events in such a way that the reader/viewer is prepared for them or can even anticipate them	
hero/heroine	→ see novel, p. 155	
irony	→ see non-fiction, p. 153	

Literary terms – drama

literary terms	definition	example
litotes	→ see non-fiction, p. 153	
mood	the feeling that the writer tries to evoke	anger, excitement, happiness, pity, sadness, …
pace	the speed at which sth. happens or is done	
plot	a series of related events that make up the main story in a book, film, etc.	
protagonist	the main character in a fictional text	
register	→ see non-fiction, p. 154	
rising action	the part of a fictional text following the exposition and leading up to the climax/turning point	
round character	→ see novel, p. 156	
scene	a part of an act in a play or film in which events happen in the same place or period of time	
script (screenplay)	a written description of a dialogue and action of a play or film, including basic camera or stage directions	
setting	the place and time at which the action of a fictional text takes place	
short plays and playlets	short in length, have few characters and usually deal with a single problem, conflict or event, which occurs in a single setting	
special effect	→ see film, p. 161	
stage directions	notes in a play telling the actors how to speak and act. They also say what the characters and the stage should look like and where and when the action takes place.	"De Clerk's mobile rings." "Tom moves over to de Clerk and massages his shoulders and neck."
static character	→ see novel, p. 156	
structure	the organisation of the elements of a text	
subtext	→ see non-fiction, 154	
suspense	a feeling of excitement or worry that makes a reader curious about the outcome of a fictional text	
symbol	→ see novel, p. 156	
tension	the feeling evoked by the conflicts of a fictional text	
tone	→ see non-fiction, p. 154	
turning point	the point at which the action takes a different, often unexpected direction	

Glossary – alphabetical

	literary terms	definition	example
A	acoustic effects	effects relating to sound, e.g. in a play or a film	
	act	one of the parts that a play is divided into. Each act is divided into two or more scenes.	Act I, scene II
	acting time	the time the action of a narrative lasts as opposed to reading time	
	action	everything that happens in a fictional text; events that form part of a play or film	In this scene, the action takes place in …
	actor/actress	the person who performs in a play or film	Jesse Eisenberg as Mark Zuckerberg in 'The Social Network'
	alliteration	emphasis that occurs through the repetition of initial consonant letters of two or more neighbouring words	"bigger box", "red rose"
	allusion	a reference to a familiar or famous historical or literary figure or event	"a King who took us to the mountaintop and pointed the way to the Promised Land" (Barack Obama refers to Martin Luther King, who explained his vision of America's future in his "I have a dream" speech.)
	anaphora	the repetition of identical words or phrases at the beginning of a sentence or a line	"Nobody hurt you. Nobody turned off the light … Nobody locked the door."
	antagonist	the main character in opposition to the protagonist of a novel	
	anti-hero	a main character in a novel or drama who does not have the qualities that a hero usually has, such as idealism or being morally good	
	antithesis/ contrast	a contrast between two things; denotes the opposing of ideas by means of grammatically parallel arrangements of words, clauses or sentences so as to produce an effective contrast	"It used to be hot, it becomes cool. It used to be strong, it becomes weak." (Malcolm X)
	antonym	a word that means the opposite of another word	night – day, wet – dry, hot – cold
	atmosphere	the feeling or mood created by the author through the description of events, setting, situation, etc.	"For a moment, a cloud drifted past the moon and the sky turned greenish gray."
B	backlighting	filming a subject or object illuminated from behind	
	bias	a prejudice in favour of or against one thing, person or group. It is a tendency to hold a certain point of view at the expense of other alternatives. An article is biased if information is presented in a one-sided way based on personal opinion rather than facts.	
C	camera range	the distance between the camera and the object filmed	
	cameraman	so. who operates a camera for making films or TV programmes	

Glossary – alphabetical

literary terms	definition	example
caption	words printed near or on a picture that explain sth. about the picture; a joke that is printed underneath a humorous drawing or photograph	
caricature	a presentation in which so.'s/sth.'s features are exaggerated to produce a comic or grotesque effect	
cast	noun: all the performers in a play or film verb: to choose an actor for a role in a play or film	
catastrophe	the unfortunate end of a story	
character	a person who takes part in the action of a fictional text	Mayor Undersee in Suzanne Collins' 'The Hunger Games'
characterization	the way in which a writer creates characters in a book, play, film etc. The author may present his characters in two ways: directly by describing them (explicit), or indirectly through their actions, thoughts or feelings and words (implicit)	"She has yellow hair, wiry legs, the most beautiful crooked smile in the world." "I was too lazy at school." "Audrey always sits opposite me, no matter where we play." → She seems to be interested
climax/crisis	the most exciting or important moment in a story, event, or situation, usually near the end. This moment determines whether the situation will improve or grow worse. *Crisis* refers to the highest point of reader interest.	
close-up	a full-screen shot of a person's face to show emotions revealed by their facial expression; it can also be used to draw attention to an object that is of particular interest to the plot or has a symbolic function.	
comic relief	a humorous scene or incident in a serious play that relieves the tension	
composer	so. who writes the music, e.g. for a film	
conclusion	the final part of a speech, an article or a piece of writing	
conflict	the disagreement between opposing forces which is the basis of the plot of a story or a play	
content	the kind of information a text contains	
crane shot	the camera is placed on a crane and moves in all directions. A crane is generally used for high angle shots.	
credits	a list of people involved in the making of a film	
cross-cutting (parallel action)	combining shots of two or more scenes which are usually taking place at the same time	
cut	a quick move from one shot to the next in a film	
D dénouement	the last part of a short story, book, play, etc. in which everything is settled	
dialogue	the words that characters speak in a fictional text, play or film	

Glossary – alphabetical

literary terms	definition	example
director (filmmaker)	so. who is in charge of making a film, or getting a play ready for performance, instructs the actors and the crew	David Fincher ('The Social Network')
drama	a work in prose or verse presenting a story which normally deals with a human conflict. It is usually intended to be acted on a stage as a play.	
dynamic character	a complex character who may change (= round character)	Manjit in Bali Rai's '(Un)arranged Marriage'
E editing (montage)	the arrangement of shots in a structured sequence	
ellipsis	leaving out words to avoid repetition	
enumeration	naming each one of a series or list of things	
establishing shot	gives an overall impression of the location at the beginning of a scene	
euphemism	a word or expression that people use when they want to talk about something unpleasant or embarrassing without mentioning the thing itself. It is used to spare the reader's feelings.	"to kick the bucket", "to fall off one's perch", "to pop one's clogs" are euphemisms of 'to die'.
exaggeration	representing (sth.) as being larger, greater, better, or worse than it really is	"We've heard this complaint a thousand times."
explicit characterization	direct characterization by the narrator (telling). The author tells the reader explicitly about the character's looks, traits, attitudes.	
exposition	the first part in a fictional text that provides background information and introduces the setting, the conflict and often the main character or character(s)	
external action	the writer describes what the characters do	"Just as the clock strikes two, the mayor steps up to the podium and begins to read."
extreme close-up (detail shot)	shows an object in detail, emphasizing its importance in the scene	
eye-level shot	the camera looks straight at the person. This may suggest a neutral view, however, it can also mean that two people who are not on the same level for some reason (e.g. wealth, age, academic standing, social class) are presented as equal to each other.	
F fade-in	if a sound or picture fades in, it gradually becomes louder or clearer	
fade-out	if a sound or picture fades out, it gradually disappears	
falling action	the part of a story or play following the crisis/climax and leading to the dénouement or catastrophe	
fiction	a piece of writing that comes from a writer's imagination. Fiction is not factual but may be sometimes based on facts, real experiences or people the writer has known.	

Glossary – alphabetical

literary terms	definition	example
field size (camera range)	the distance between the camera and the object filmed	
film	a series of moving pictures with sound that you can watch at the cinema or on television.	
flashback	a scene that shows what happened in the past and thus interrupts the chronological order of the plot	
flashforward	a scene that shows what may happen in the future and thus interrupts the chronological order of the plot	
flat character	a character who does not develop in the course of the action and is often a stereotype (= static character)	Harry in Bali Rai's '(Un)arranged Marriage'
focal point	the central point in a cartoon which is of interest	
foreshadowing	the technique of hinting at future events in such a way that the reader/viewer is prepared for them or can even anticipate them	
full shot	gives a view of the entire figure of a person to show action or to give an impression of a constellation of characters	
genre	a particular style used in cinema or writing which can be recognized by certain features, such as subject matter, theme, type of characters, etc	novel, poem, short story, drama
hand-held camera (handy cam)	the cameraman holds the camera in his hand when filming. This conveys a feeling of authenticity to the viewer.	
heading	a title at the top of a page or a piece of writing	
headline	the title of a cartoon, a newspaper story, etc.	
hero/heroine	the main character, protagonist, who usually has good qualities	Katniss Everdeen in Suzanne Collins' 'The Hunger Games'
high angle shot	the camera looks down on the object so that it seems smaller, less important or inferior	
imagery	use of vivid or descriptive language to represent objects, actions or ideas	
implicit characterization	indirect characterization through action, behaviour, words, feelings and thoughts (showing). You learn a lot about a character by studying what he says and does, how he behaves in certain situations and interacts with others.	"Audrey always sits opposite me, no matter where we play." → She seems to be interested.
internal action	the writer shows the thoughts and feelings of the characters	"… but Grace felt a smile cracking her face."
introduction	the part at the beginning of any text (exposition)	
irony	the reversal of the normal order of words	"In fact, it was his last big joke before his sense of humour calcified and had to be removed."

Glossary – alphabetical

literary terms	definition	example
J jump cut	a cut between two pictures leaving out some action	
L lighting	refers to the illumination of a camera subject being filmed. The lighting may be natural or artificial, very bright (high-key lighting) or dark (low-key lighting).	
litotes	understatement, making sth./so. less important than in reality	"She's not as young as she was." = She's old.
long shot	provides a view of the situation or setting from a distance	
low angle shot	the camera looks up at a person so that people seem more important, powerful or even intimidating as it shows them in a superior position	
M main part/body	the body/main part of a book or document, not including the introduction or the notes	
match cut	two scenes that are connected by visual or acoustic means, e.g. a door is closed in one scene and opened in the following scene in a different context, someone is crying at the end of the first and the beginning of the second scene	
medium long shot	shows a person or people in interaction with their surroundings	
medium shot	shows a person down to the waist, often used to present two people in conversation	
metaphor	two ideas that are normally not linked are compared in a metaphor without using "as" or "like". This creates an image in the reader's mind and makes the description more powerful.	"They blazed a trail toward freedom through the darkest of nights." (Barack Obama)
mood	the feeling that the writer tries to evoke	excitement, anger, sadness, happiness, pity, …
N narrative	any writing that tells a story	
narrator	a fictitious person who tells the story in a novel or film	
non-fiction	texts that give facts about real events, things or people	
novel	a fairly long fictional prose narrative. Normally it has a plot which develops through the actions, speech, and thoughts of its characters.	
O omniscient narrator	a narrator knowing everything about the characters	
open ending	a structural element in fictional texts in which the conflict remains for the most part unresolved	
overhead shot (bird's eye view)	makes an object seem less important, or gives orientation	
over-the-shoulder shot	often used to present two people in conversation. You are looking straight at one person from behind the second person.	

Glossary – alphabetical

literary terms	definition	example
P pace	the speed at which sth. happens or is done	
pan (panning shot)	the camera moves horizontally, i.e. to the left or to the right as opposed to tilting	
paradox	a statement consisting of two parts that seem to mean the opposite of each other	"I can resist anything but temptation." (Oscar Wilde)
paragraph	a section of a piece of writing that begins on a new line and contains a group of several interrelated sentences	
parallelism	the repetition of sentence pattern often used to contrast	"… look at you. Look at us …"
personification	the presentation of ideas, objects or animals as persons to make them more interesting for the reader	"That carrot cake with the cream cheese icing is calling my name."
perspective	the point of view from which a story is presented. The story can be told by a first-person or by a third-person narrator. The narrator can be a character in or outside the story. The third-person narrator can be omniscient (knowing everything about the characters) or limited (perceiving and knowing the same things as one character, seeing through the eyes of one character).	first-person perspective third-person perspective: omiscient or limited
play	a play is literature written for the stage	
plot	a series of related events that make up the main story in a book, film, etc.	
point of view	the relation in which the narrator stands to the story, a mental viewpoint or attitude	
point-of-view shot	assumes the perspective of one of the characters so that we seem to look through his eyes	
producer	the person who is responsible for the financing and marketing of a film	
production designer	the person who designs the set for scenes that are shot in the studio	
protagonist	the main character in a fictional text	Winston Smith in George Orwell's '1984'
R reading time	the time it takes a person to read the story (as opposed to acting time)	
register	the level of language (degree of formality)	formal, informal, slang, …
repetition	words or phrases that are used more than once in a text, catching the reader's attention	"She knew this though: she loved kites and she loved rainbows. And, above all, she loved her mother."
reverse-angle shot	a sequence of point-of-view shots in which the perspective changes from one speaker to the other	
review	a report in a newspaper or magazine in which a critic gives his views of a new film, novel, etc.	
rhetorical question	a question which expects no answer	"What does it matter now?"

Glossary – alphabetical

literary terms	definition	example
rising action	the part of a fictional text following the exposition and leading to the climax/turning point	
round character	a complex character who may change (= dynamic character)	Manjit in Bali Rai's '(Un)arranged Marriage'
scene	a part of an act in a play or film in which events happen in the same place or period of time	
script (screenplay)	a written description of the dialogue and action of a play or film, including basic camera directions	
scriptwriter	the person who writes the text for a film	
sequence	a series of scenes which belong together	
setting	the place and time at which the action of a fictional text takes place	
short plays and playlets	short in length, have few characters and usually deal with a single problem, conflict or event, which occurs in a single setting	
short story	a work of fiction which usually deals with one or two major characters and one major conflict. The elements of a short story are character, plot, setting and theme.	
shot	a length of film without a break; the smallest structural unit of a film	
simile	a comparison of two ideas, often linked by "as" or "like"	"Like a magic kingdom that belonged only to Grace and her mother."
sound designer	the person who creates special sounds for a film	
sound recordist	the person who records the dialogue spoken by the actors	
sound technician	the person in charge of a film's soundtrack	
soundtrack	all the recorded sound of a film (dialogue, sound and sound effects)	
special effect	an unusual image or sound that has been produced artificially	
stage directions	notes in a play telling the actors how to speak and act. They also say what the characters and the stage should look like and where and when the action takes place.	"De Clerk's mobile rings." "Tom moves over to de Clerk and massages his shoulders and neck."
static character	a character who does not develop in the course of the action and is often a stereotype (= flat character)	Effie Trinket in Suzanne Collins' 'The Hunger Games'
static shot	the camera does not move	
still	a photograph taken from one of the scenes in a film	
storyboard	a series of pictures that the director of a film uses to plan the action that will be filmed	

Glossary – alphabetical

literary terms	definition	example
straight-on angle (eye-level shot)	the camera looks straight at the person. This may suggest a neutral view, however, it can also mean that two people who are not on the same level for some reason (e.g. wealth, age, academic standing, social class) are presented as equal to each other.	
stream of consiousness	the thoughts of a character in a book that are expressed as they happen	
structure	the organisation of the elements of a text	
style	the special, often personal and individual way in which a writer expresses ideas depending on personal factors and the type of text he/she is writing	
stylistic devices	techniques used to convince the reader/listener of the author's idea	repetition, enumeration, irony, exaggeration, metaphor, tone
sub-heading	the title of one section of a longer piece of writing	
sub-plot	a plot that is subordinate to the main plot of a literary work	
subtext	the hidden meaning in a conversation, not expressed by words, but by intonation, tone of voice, facial expression, gesture, posture	
suspense	a feeling of excitement or worry that makes a reader curious about the outcome of a fictional text	
symbol	an image that does not only stand for itself but also signifies a more abstract concept or idea	"Baby steps have a way of adding up to a lot of big steps."
synchronisation	the technique of matching the sound with the image	
tension	the feeling evoked by the conflicts of a fictional text	
theme	the main idea the writer wants to present. As the theme is usually not stated directly, the reader has to figure it out.	
tilt (tilting shot)	the camera moves vertically, i.e. upwards or downwards as opposed to panning	
tone	the tone the author uses to convey his/her attitude towards the subject	ironic, sarcastic, serious, sentimental, humorous
tracking shot	the camera follows a person or an object	
trailer	a short filmed advertisement for a film	
transcript	the storyboard and complete dialogue of a film	
turning point	the point at which the action takes a different, often unexpected direction	
voice-off	the speaker is shown in the picture	
voice-on	the speaker is not shown in the picture	
voice-over	the voice of a narrator commenting on what is being shown	
zoom in/zoom out	a stationary camera seems to move closer to or further away from the object, hereby focussing on it or showing it in its surroundings	

Copyrights

Bildquellenverzeichnis

Umschlag: Getty Images, München/The Image Bank/Lucas Lenie Photo
S. 6: Cover zu Simon Hoggart und Emily Monk: "Don't tell Mum"
S. 7: D.C. Thomson & Co., Dundee, Scotland
S. 8: Sean Smith, Guardian News & Media Limited
S. 15: Mike Buscher, Baltimore, USA
S. 18: http://www.bbc.co.uk/news/education-11509722
S. 22: Au Pair World, Kassel
S. 23: Joerg Boethling photography, Hamburg
S. 24: iStockphoto.com, Calgary (quavondo)
S. 31: *(1)* action press, Hamburg (Wallrath), *(2)* Fabian, Michael, Hannover, *(3)* Druwe & Polastri, Cremlingen/Weddel, *(4)* alamy images, Abingdon/Oxfordshire (David R. Frazier Photolibrary, Inc.), *(5)* fotolia.com, New York (Kadmy), *(6)* Shutterstock.com, New York (visi.stock), *(7)* Picture-Alliance GmbH, Frankfurt/M. (Jiang ren), *(8)* Corbis, Berlin (Orjan F. Ellingvag/Dagens Naringsliv
S. 32: *(1)* dreamstime.com, Brentwood, *(2, 4)* Picture-Alliance GmbH, Frankfurt/M. (united-archives/mcphoto, Britta Pedersen), *(3)* fotolia.com, New York
S. 39: fotolia.com, New York
S. 40, 41: dreamstime.com, Brentwood
S. 42: fotolia.com, New York
S. 44: Berliner Zeitung, Berlin (Markus Wächter)
S. 48: *(1)* akg-images GmbH, Berlin (O. Martel), *(2)* alamy images, Abingdon/Oxfordshire (Lumi Images); Picture-Alliance GmbH, Frankfurt/M. *(3)* (EPA/O. Mattheys, *(4)* (Fotoagentur KUNZ), *(5)* (Bildagentur Huber/R. Schmid), *(6)* (Tom Maelsa)
S. 49: *(7)* Picture-Alliance GmbH, Frankfurt/M. (Denkou Images), *(8)* Picture-Alliance GmbH, Frankfurt/M. (ZB/S. Sauer), *(9)* Picture-Alliance GmbH, Frankfurt/M. (Marius Becker), *(10)* alamy images, Abingdon/Oxfordshire (Edward Simons),
S. 50: Cover zu Bali Rai: "(Un)arranged Marriage"
S. 60: Cartoon Stock Ltd, Bath
S. 62: Meiklejohn Graphics, London (Griff)
S. 64: *(1)* Cartoon Stock Ltd, Bath; *(2)* Whyatt, Tim, South Australia; (3+4) © Randy Glasbergen
S. 67: Cartoon Stock Ltd, Bath
S. 71: from TIME Magazine (27.12.2010) © TIME magazine. All rights reserved.
S. 74: *(1, 6)* alamy images, Oxfordshire, *(2, 7)* Picture Press, Hamburg, *(3, 5, 8)* Cinetext, Frankfurt/Main; *(4)* Picture-Alliance, Frankfurt/Main
S. 81: © Randy Glasbergen
S. 98: Gleason, Rachel
S. 100: Cover zu Margaret Atwood: "The Handmaid's Tail"; Cover zu Kazuo Ishiguro: "Never let me go"
S. 101: Cover zu Michael Grant: "Gone"; Cover zu Dave Eggers: "The Circle"
S. 102: Scholastic Inc., New York
S. 107: Cover zu George Orwell: "1984"
S. 111: iStockphoto.com, Calgary
S. 112: Asian Development Bank (ADB), Mandaluyong City
S. 113: H & M HENNES & MAURITZ B.V. & Co. KG , Hamburg
S. 115: Getty Images, München (Bloomberg)
S. 120: iStockphoto.com, Calgary (ajt)
S. 122: Methling, Inga, Köln
S. 134: Cartoon Stock Ltd, GB-Bath (Plenderleith, Allan)

Textquellenverzeichnis

S. 6-7: three emails from "Don't tell Mum" © Simon Hoggart and Emily Monk, The Random House, UK, 2007.
S. 8-9: from "Gap years: Wasted youth?" by Patrick Kingsley, in The *Guardian*, 06.09.2010, © Guardian News & Media Ltd 2014.
S. 15-17: from "Gap year before college gives grads valuable life experience" © G. Jeffrey MacDonald, 18.06.2008
S. 32-33: from "Top tips for Skype interviews" on *guardianjobs* (online), © Guardian News & Media Ltd 2014.
S. 44-47: from "Kein Privatleben, aber sehr gute Aussichten" by Barbara Weitzel in the Berliner Zeitung, 24.02.2014, © 2014 Berliner Zeitung
S. 50-51: from "(Un)arranged Marriage" © Bali Rai, published by Corgi. Reprinted by permission of The Random House Group Ltd, London, 2001. S. 15–18
S. 58-59: from "Guantanamo Boy" © Anna Perera, 2009, pp.24-26.
S. 60-61: from "Amy" © Mary Hooper, Bloomsbury: New York and London, 2002.
S. 61: from "Fever of the Bone" © Val McDermid, HarperCollins Publishers: New York, 2009.
S. 65: "NJ student's suicide illustrates Internet dangers" by Geoff Mulvihill und Samantha Henry, in *The Washington Post*, 01.10.2010. The Associated Press Copyright © 2010. All rights reserved.
S. 68-69: "How dangerous is the Internet for children?" by David Pogue, from *The New York Times*, (28.02.2008) © The New York Times. All rights reserved. Used by permission and protected by the Copyright Laws oft the United States. The printing, copying, redistribution, or retransmission of this Content without express written permission is prohibited.
S. 71: from "Will Facebook conquer the world?" by Shane Richmond and Will Heaven, in *The Telegraph*, 04.01.2011. © Telegraph Media Group Limited 2011.
S. 78: from "Hot or not? Website briefly judges looks" © Bari M. Schwartz, 04.11.2003.
S. 79: from "Person of the year 2010: Facebook's Mark Zuckerman" by Lev Grossmann, in *TIME magazine*, (27.12.2010) © TIME magazine. All rights reserved.
S. 82: "11 Reasons to quit Facebook in 2014" by Renee Jacques, in The *Huffington Post*, 30.12.2013.
S. 82: "Teenagers tell researchers it's a cruel, cruel online world" by Somini Sengupta, in The *New York Times*, 09.11.2011.
S. 84: from "Facebook: 10 years of trying to be liked" by Hannah Slapper, in The *Guardian*, 03.02.2014, © Guardian News & Media Ltd 2014.
S. 85: from "How Facebook changed our lives" by Marco della Cava, in *USA Today*, 02.02.2014.
S. 86: from "Still on Facebook, but finding less to like" by Jenna Wortham, in The *New York Times*, 16.11.2013.
S. 87: from "Seeing Social Media more as portal than as pitfall" by Perri Klass, in The *New York Times*, 09.01.2012.
S. 88: from "Citizenship" by Mark Ravenhill, in *Shell connections 2005: New plays for young people*, faber & faber: London, 2005, S. 219–220. © Mark Ravenhill, Citizenship and Methuen Drama, an imprint of Bloomsbury Publishing Plc.
S. 90-92: from "A Vampire Story" © Moira Buffini, in *New connections 2008: Plays for young people*, faber & faber: London, 2008, S. 478–483.
S. 98: from "The Living Room: Identity and acceptance in West Michigan's LGBT community" by Stateside Staff, on *Michigan Radio*, 10.03.2014.
S. 102, 105: from "The Hunger Games" by Suzanne Collins, Scholastic pp. 19-24
S. 108-109: from "1984" by George Orwell, Penguin, pp.7-10
S. 115-116: from "Why I'm Not Excited About H&M's Australian Launch" by Maddie Newman on Junkee, 07.04.2014
S. 120: "Upcyling industry takes a bite out of national waste stream" by Chris Long on *pandodaily*, 16.12.2013
S. 122: "Tausende bei Primark Eröffnung" by Corinna Schulz in the *Kölner Stadtanzeiger*, 02.05.2014